AMERICAN
THEMES

American Themes

SELECTED ESSAYS AND ADDRESSES OF

JOHN ALLEN KROUT

EDITED BY

CLIFFORD LORD AND HENRY F. GRAFF

Columbia University Press

NEW YORK AND LONDON 1963

Preface

JOHN ALLEN KROUT is now turning another corner of his life. He is entering what used to be called "retirement," a period in modern American life often more hectic than any which went before, for him a third stage in what has been called "sequential careers."

In the pages which follow, the editors have gathered a selection of John Krout's writings and speeches, published and unpublished, which to them best exhibit the man: the social historian of his country, the able writer, the deeply moralistic teacher. But because a man is only partially mirrored in his writings, it is appropriate to sketch first the facts of his careers as historian and teacher and as academic administrator in order to suggest the full dimensions of an unusual character and personality.

Owing to the design of this book, documentary citations have been omitted. Our purpose is to introduce the reader to the mind and heart of John Allen Krout, not to exhibit his skill with footnotes. For the speeches, no footnotes exist. For the historical articles or chapters, they are available in the original printed versions.

We are indebted to many people for assistance in the preparation of this volume: to John Hastings of the Columbia News Office, Helen Gerberich, formerly of the *Political Science Quarterly*, and Herbert Kahler of the National Park Service, for suggesting several otherwise unknown manuscripts; to Constance M. Winchell and her colleagues in the reference division of the Columbia University Libraries for the bibliography and for many special services; to the numerous friends around the country who conspired with us to circumvent by tape recordings the well-known Krout propensity for delivering extemporaneous speeches; to John himself for being the sort of person he is, thus making the preparation of this volume a genuine pleasure.

CLIFFORD LORD
HENRY F. GRAFF

Columbia University
June, 1963

Contents

viii   CONTENTS

Y O U *have seen many changes on Morningside in the course of your long association with Columbia. If they are good, it is in no small part because you have helped to make them so. With unfailing good humor, patience, and that quality of judgment of men and events that can only be summed up as* wisdom, *you have dealt most effectively with all the myriad problems that have crossed your desk. It is not as easy to be firm yet kindly, but you have shown us all that it can be done and we have profited from the example.*

GRAYSON KIRK TO JOHN ALLEN KROUT

Introduction

"'HE's all Columbia"—this simple phrase is the highest compliment in John Krout's abundant vocabulary. It is, moreover, an important key to understanding the author of the pages which follow, for aside from a few months in business in the unsettled year following his graduation from the University of Michigan in 1918, Columbia University has been the matrix of his life.

John Krout first saw the campus the summer after graduation from the Monroe Street Grammar School in Tiffin, Ohio. His father, Charles Allen Krout—for most of his long and full career Tiffin's superintendent of schools and professor of American history and civics to senior students—that summer brought his older son, John, and one of John's classmates for brief visits to Boston, Washington, and New York before undertaking himself a summer's work at Teachers College. A few years later the son declined a fellowship at Harvard, went instead to Columbia (without a scholarship), expecting to study law. There Harlan Fiske Stone perceived his prospective student's true bent—initially shaped at Michigan by the late Robert Treat Crane—and dispatched him to Professors William A. Dunning and Carlton J. H. Hayes of the Faculty of Political

Science. From that moment in the fall of 1919 on, John Allen Krout has been "all Columbia": graduate student, fellow, assistant, teacher in Columbia's premedical program at the Long Island Medical School (later Seth Low Junior College), instructor in University Classes, head of history in Extension, professor, departmental chairman, acting director of the School of General Studies, dean of the graduate faculties, associate provost, provost and vice-president—the post he left on terminal leave, April 1, 1962.

At Columbia he has first of all been a teacher. "Great" is not a word for light or careless use, but John Krout is a great teacher. For 27 years—from 1921 to 1948—his classroom lectures, delivered with notable vigor, held spellbound his Columbia undergraduate and graduate students. No one ever more successfully brought to life the discussions of the Constitutional Convention, the Hayne-Webster debate, the reforms and reformers of the 1840's, as he bestrode the lecture hall *sans* notes. Clay was in one corner, Calhoun in another, Webster in another, as Krout, jaw outthrust, finger pointing, with an oratory to match their best, played out the Compromise of 1850 role by role. A short man, he seemed tall. In the seminar, he radiated a kindly cordiality until a shoddy performance roused the famous temper to Old Testament wrath or quiet vivisection. He kindled lasting enthusiasms and admiration. And of his many seminarians who entered college teaching, each unquestionably took with him some small part of the techniques of the master.

His talent as a speaker had long been nurtured. In high school at Tiffin he twice made the debating team and was valedictorian of his class. At Heidelberg College he debated during all three years. And when, on the advice of one of his professors, he transferred for greater intellectual stimulation to the University of Michigan for his senior year, he again made the team. At Michigan Professor Thomas C. Trueblood, coach of debating, added memorably to his earlier training and to the inspiration of an admired uncle, the Reverend Theodore Bacher. A remarkable forensic ability, a sure and unfailing touch for the apt quotation or the appropriate anecdote, a memory which made notes superfluous, and a resonant and appealing voice were combined to create an unusually effective classroom teacher and a platform lecturer in wide demand.

The teaching years brought great satisfactions and widespread recognition. A summer assistantship with David Saville Muzzey prefaced later collaboration on the Muzzey and Krout college text. Curricula in both European and American history for Columbia's experiment in home study were prepared, the former with J. Lloyd Mecham (later with John H. Wuorinen), the latter with Roy F. Nichols. Subsequently he prepared the outline books on American history for the Barnes and Noble series, one of which—on recent United States history—is currently in its 14th edition. His Ph.D. thesis (1925), *The Origins of Prohibition,* was published by Knopf, and a chapter accepted for *The American Mercury* by H. L. Mencken. *The Outlook* (1927) published his one-page appraisals of the roles of the several founding fathers in the establishment of the nation for its national oratorical contest. He contributed 16 sketches of prominent New Yorkers to the *Dictionary of American Biography,* the sketch of Neal Dow to the *Encyclopedia of the Social Sciences,* and for three years (1925–27) the article on American political history to the *American Yearbook.* With Dixon Ryan Fox, he wrote *The Completion of Independence* for the *History of American Life* series. He authored the volume on sports (v. 15) for the *Pageant of America* and contributed two chapters to the multi-volume *History of the State of New York.* The bibliography which concludes this volume records his other work in social, localized New York, and early national history. He reviewed for the *American Historical Review,* the *New York Times Book Review,* the *Historical Outlook,* the *Saturday Review,* the *Yale Review, New York History,* and other journals. In December, 1936, he succeeded Parker T. Moon as managing editor of both the *Proceedings* of the Academy of Political Science and the *Political Science Quarterly.*

Close friendship with Dixon Ryan Fox led to a lasting interest in New York history and in the New York State Historical Association. Elected a trustee in 1935— and reelected ever since—he has rendered particularly valuable service on the publications committee, in the selection of the last three directors of the Association, and after Dr. Fox's untimely death in 1946, on the committee to establish and administer the Fox Memorial Fund. Previously, after Fox had become president of Union College in 1934, Dr. Krout declined an urgent offer of a full professorship at Union years before he could expect that rank at Columbia. His loyalty to his University was firmly established. He knew, to his own satisfaction, where his life's work lay.

In 1938 he received the first of a number of honorary

degrees—an L.H.D. from his old college, Heidelberg. Two years later he was elected president of the Middle States Association of History Teachers and in 1942 his colleagues named him chairman of the Department of History for the first of three terms. In 1944 he became secretary of the Society of American Historians.

To the volunteer rejected by the Navy in World War I (at 99 pounds, he was underweight), World War II brought added professional responsibilities. When Franklin D. Roosevelt ordered all war agencies to keep histories of their activities, the Social Science Research Council set up a Committee on War History Studies. Here John Krout served with his close friend of graduate school days, Roy Nichols of the University of Pennsylvania, with Pendleton Herring, James Phinney Baxter, and others, guiding the program, recruiting able young historians to undertake the departmental assignments, and shepherding to completion a host of volumes, many of which have appeared in print and many of which are still classified for departmental use only.

In 1944 when the operational histories of the Air Force, conceived on a gargantuan scale by Col. Clanton Williams, appeared to be bogging down in an unmanageable mass of paper, John Krout was one of the experts named to review the program, to establish ground rules governing the selective preservation of source materials, and, as one member of the committee put it, "to interpret Clanton Williams to General Arnold."

Three years later the board of the Museum of the City of New York, made acutely aware by Robert Moses, who was then Park Commissioner, of growing public concern over apparent duplication of efforts between its operation and that of the nearby but far older New-York Historical Society, called on John Krout for recommendations. The Krout survey basically recommended that the museum stress its museum function, leave manuscripts and library to the New-York Historical Society. His findings, confirmed in a subsequent policy survey nearly a decade later, resulted in his election to the Museum's board, on which he served from 1948 to 1962.

The second career began shortly before his fifty-second birthday, as John Allen Krout moved from classroom to administration. Grayson Kirk was chairman, John Krout vice-chairman of the committee in charge of the inauguration on June 7, 1948, of Dwight D. Eisenhower as president of the University. The efficiency with which the event was conducted (and in John Krout's case, a speech at the opening dinner of the Men's Faculty Club) brought both men to the pleased attention of the new president, and both were shortly brought into administration. The sudden death of Harry Morgan Ayres, first director of the School of General Studies (Columbia's then new college for adults), created the vacancy to which the neophyte president, at the suggestion of Albert C. Jacobs, then provost, called the chairman of the history department. The following year (March, 1949), with the strong support of Dean Harry J. Carman of Columbia College, he was named dean of the graduate faculties. Grayson Kirk became provost a few months later, and Krout was named associate provost (a position he held in addition to his post as dean of the graduate faculties). When President Eisenhower left for SHAPE soon thereafter, the administration of the University fell largely to the provost and vice-president (Kirk) and to the associate provost and dean of the graduate faculties (Krout). In January, 1953, Kirk succeeded to the presidency, and two months later John Krout became provost and vice-president. He relinquished the post of provost in 1958.

This is not the place to appraise John Krout's many services to the University in these successive offices: not his work as graduate dean in ending the printing requirements for the doctoral thesis, strengthening the Ph.D. program for Teachers College students under the Joint Committee on Graduate Instruction, or obtaining more scholarship money, all the while conferring with students, building good will for the University. Nor his role in the celebration of the University Bicentennial (1954), where he served as chairman of the publications committee, gave a great many speeches, chaired the October conference on the unity of knowledge at Arden House. Nor his part in the development and implementation of the program for the educational future of the University (the MacMahon Committee); his sharing of the fund raising, administrative, speaking, and social duties of the presidency; his quite spectacular services as greeter of distinguished visitors.

It is, however, the logical place to characterize his qualities as administrator. For John Krout is a man of monumental integrity—forthright, honest, sincere. There has never been any question where he stood—often arms akimbo—on an issue. Or why. One might disagree, but one knew his position and his reasons for it—a rarity among administrators particularly, perhaps, in the academic world. Presiding in committee, or in faculty meeting, he was usually the personification of patience, offering everyone the chance to be heard yet displaying a rare knack to move to decision before deliberation degenerated into general discussion.

Off campus, his services to his University were many and varied. World War II brought rent control. Neighborhood landlords, caught between fixed rents and rising costs—and with an eye to greater profits—subdivided apartments, often one family to a room with no change in basic facilities. Slums burgeoned around the campus, creating problems which immensely complicated life for university administrators. When the city and the federal government designated Manhattanville, a section of nearby west Harlem, as one of the early Title One slum-clearance projects, the Rev. Harry Emerson Fosdick of the Riverside Church proposed a special social work program known as the Manhattanville Neighborhood Center. Most of the neighboring institutions joined as sponsors—Columbia in 1949, two years after the project was launched. From this undertaking stemmed the Community Services Committee, created in 1956. From it also emerged the establishment of Morningside Heights, Inc., which has moved in many ways to reverse the visible deterioration of the neighborhood, to halt the flight of the faculty to the suburbs, and to recreate a resident community of scholars at Morningside Heights. In all the time-consuming negotiations and meetings these and less productive proposals demanded, John Krout, from 1949 on, represented Columbia. He was on the board of Manhattanville Community Centers, Inc., chairman of the Community Services Committee, on the board of Morningside Heights, Inc.

John Krout maintained his professional interests despite the heavy demands of his administrative posts. He resigned the editorship of the *Political Science Quarterly* in 1953 but remained active in the Academy of Political Science and the American Historical Association. In 1947 he joined the board of the Institute of Early American History and Culture. When the American History Research Center was established at Madison, Wisconsin, in 1950, he was one of the nationally known Americanists named to its advisory council. And when its work was taken over by the American Association for State and Local History in 1961, he carried on as a member of the Research and Publication Committee.

Understandably, John Krout was interested in the preservation of Alexander Hamilton's Grange, one of the few buildings of the Revolutionary period still standing in the city. It had been saved by the American Scenic and Historic Preservation Society, but was falling into disrepair for lack of funds. At one time he tried in vain to bring it to the Columbia campus, for Hamilton had been a student at King's (later Columbia) College. Through these efforts he became a friend of the present Alexander Hamilton and active in the American Scenic and Historic Preservation Society.

Some years later John Krout was brought in as advisor to the National Park Service and then as chairman of the Historians Committee on the projected Immigration Museum for Bedloe's Island, another project in which Mr.

Hamilton was deeply interested. And in the compilation and publication of the Papers of Alexander Hamilton, Dr. Krout—with Charles G. Proffitt of the Columbia University Press—was one of the moving spirits.

In 1957 John Krout was named to the Advisory Board of the National Park Service. This board, created to help the staff maintain high standards in the designation of national monuments and historic sites, was soon immersed in the major historical surveys, region by region, of significant sites which were part of the Mission 66 program. The only academic historian on the board, Krout quickly became chairman of the committee on history, materially helped guide this huge governmental research program to successful conclusion. And in 1959 he collaborated with a colleague and former student, Henry F. Graff, on a notable high school text, *The Adventure of the American People.*

But there is more to John Allen Krout than the social historian, the great teacher, the frank and effective administrator, the man devoted to his University.

He who would understand John Krout must know and understand the Midwest. Here at Tiffin, Ohio, 40 miles south of Put-in-Bay, he was born on October 3, 1896. His educator-father imparted to him an earnest faith in the perfectability of mankind through education. The family, and undoubtedly the community, gave him a sure sense of morality and a firm grounding in basic Christian beliefs and ethics. The Midwesterner is proverbially open-hearted and easy to meet. John Krout was not only a collegiate debater, but manager of the football team at Heidelberg, class president his sophomore year,

editor both of the college newspaper and annual. And
ever since he has been the genial, almost jovial, ready
acquaintance—good company, despite a deep inner re-
serve which few, if any, have penetrated.

The deeply rooted religious element in his character
found him, even as a graduate student at Columbia, teaching Sunday school to a group of teen-age boys at the
Mt. Morris Baptist Church. When the family moved to
suburban Scarsdale, he continued this Sunday morning
devotion at the Hitchcock Memorial Church. And after
the Krouts returned to Morningside Heights, he became
in 1951 a trustee of the Riverside Church. Here he served
on many committees—executive, house, support and interpretation, stewardship and salary, but most importantly
as chairman of the building committee responsible for the
construction of the South Wing.

He is and has been deeply loyal and devoted to his
family. On September 15, 1923, he married Marion D.
Good, of Bellevue, Ohio. Warm, cordial, gracious, ebul-
lient, she was a delightful hostess, and like her husband
excellent company. Thirty-six years of happy married
companionship ensued, the last fourteen of which were
darkened by the wife's invalidism. During these years the
husband gave up practically all outside engagements, except those at which he represented his University, in
order to spend as much time as possible at her side. His
devotion to her was matched by that for his remarkable
father and for his younger brother, who died tragically
young in 1957. The tribulations of his own generation
were increasingly offset by the younger part of the family: his vivacious and devoted daughter, Eleanor (Mrs.

Gerald M. Bache), born in 1925, and three bouyant grandchildren whose development increasingly intrigued and supported the grandfather. And then just a few months before he entered his present hectic "retirement" he remarried, the bride also being an Ohioan, Mary Pryseski, another delightful lady, a talented singer and long an associate in the office of the graduate dean and later of the provost and vice-president.

Numerous honors have come to John Krout: honorary membership in Phi Beta Kappa, decorations from the Venezuelan and Italian governments, honorary degrees from Union College (1952), Washington and Jefferson (1954), Hamilton (1957), John Carroll (1962), Columbia (1963), a trusteeship at Smith College (1961), board membership at the Empire City Savings Bank and the Atran Foundation, the Alexander Hamilton Medal of the Columbia College Alumni Association. More will follow.

But the greatest honor that can come to any man is already his: the deep, abiding admiration and affection not just of a few but of the many—former students, colleagues at Columbia, associates in his many professional and civic undertakings, and indeed the thousands who have come within sight and sound of his warming personality and his resonant oratory. Those of us fortunate enough to have known him well wish here to record and acknowledge our high esteem for John Allen Krout of Columbia University.

C.L.
H.F.G.

≺ I ≻

MAIN THEMES
IN AMERICAN HISTORY

THE *broadgauged generalization and pithy phrase to give it force are principal characteristics of John Krout's exceptional skill. His presentations of the meaning of America profoundly move and edify a vast variety of audiences with equal effect—undergraduates and graduate students, members of professional societies, and the public at large. Invariably he combines the forensic art with a deeply felt mastery of historical materials.*

This opening selection is a forceful analysis of the main themes in the history of John Krout's America. One of ten lectures delivered by Columbia professors to members of the United Nations Secretariat, it was presented informally at International House, New York City, February 14, 1948.

Main Themes
in American History

IT is not an easy thing to discuss with citizens of the United States the course of their own historical development. I've found that out in the last twenty-five years. How much more difficult it is to discuss the subject with you who are from distant lands and from widely different backgrounds.

American history has so many themes that any one who tries to select the most important of them will probably be regarded as either foolish or ignorant. I am going to take that risk this morning. The main theme of American history, inclusive of all others, is the conquest of a large part of the North American continent by immigrants from Europe and Africa and Asia.

It was a heroic conquest accomplished by the very hard work of men and of women—let that be emphasized—within the relatively narrow span of less than three centuries. On the military side, to be sure, it pales in comparison with the conquests of the Roman legions, and yet, was mankind ever offered quite so freely such breath-taking opportunities? The central fact is the new continent, its size, its natural resources, its tremendous power to sustain human life. We cannot repeat to ourselves too often the truth that the only thing new about Americans was America.

Here then is the principal theme, the transit of civilization from the Old World to the New. Much has been written about the physical characteristics of the migrations in the seventeenth and eighteenth centuries, about the Anglo-Saxons and the Scotch-Irish, the Dutch and the Germans, the French and the Spanish, the Swiss and the Celtic Irish, and the African who came by the tens of thousands to these shores. We have studied the motives that lay behind their coming, their religious interests, their love of adventure, their desire for wealth—"Gospel, glory, gold" one of my colleagues at Columbia used to call it. But we have only begun to understand, at least so it seems to me, the more important parts of the story: what they brought with them in their mental baggage, what they deeply cherished when they set foot on these shores, how they contrived over several centuries to establish here the learned professions, the arts and sciences, the specialties and refinements that grow out of their intelligently living together. That is the story we have only begun to understand.

One example can throw some light on this process of transit. How, for instance, did the American family doctor get here? There were a few herb doctors and leeches, as you might call them, in the seventeenth-century migration to America. They practiced their healing art very crudely. Whether it was because they killed so many upon whom they practiced, or because they inspired young native-born Americans, gradually a small group began to say: "Let us go back to Europe and study where some of these practitioners ought to have studied longer." By the eighteenth century a small but continuing stream of American-born young men were going back to learn from the practitioners at Edinburgh or at Leyden. Toward the end of the eighteenth century, a few even ventured to Paris to see whether there they could master the intricacies of medicine.

They came back to practice here in the English colonies in America. They began to establish medical schools —the first one at Philadelphia, the second here in New York in connection with the little college known then as King's College. They still had to rely in large part for the teachers who staffed those small schools upon men who had had European training. Sometimes they brought distinguished Europeans over to stay for a few years to help them. But with the passing of the decades, they began to establish their own medical schools, and by the time the Revolutionary War was finished and the new nation was beginning its independent existence, they felt able to train physicians here in the United States who could go out and practice and teach others, so that it would no longer be necessary to return to Europe to learn the competence which Europeans had given to an earlier generation of American youth.

That, it seems to me, is the pattern—a pattern which several decades ago the late Dixon Ryan Fox so ably demonstrated in his writings on American social history. It is a pattern which you can apply very readily to the law, to teaching, to scientific development, to pictorial and plastic art, and to music.

The generation at the end of the American Revolution

had not completely achieved success in every one of these fields, but it could say that it was now prepared to to see how well it could carry these arts and sciences, these professional competencies, into the newer communities that lay beyond the Appalachian Mountains. It was a generation, in other words, that was beginning to feel that it had passed through the first stages along the road toward cultural maturity. It had not arrived, but it was on the way.

There is another fact about that generation at the end of the American Revolution that we can never forget: the fact that it was not only going to carry the attributes of civilization into a newer western region but also that it was going to be able to work out some novel ideas in the process.

Americans had lived for a century and three-quarters as colonials within an expanding British Empire. They were now free from those political restraints. They were on their own. But even more important, they possessed an imperial domain waiting to be settled. It must have staggered them a little bit as they said in the 1780's and 1790's: "What are we going to do with these lands that are our colonies and that fortunately, unlike most colonies, are not located across the sea thousands of miles away from us, but lie veritably at our own back door? We do not get there by taking a long sea voyage, after which we have to begin to reclaim a wilderness. We get there by steadily pushing the thin edge of civilization into areas where no European or Asiatic or African has ever yet settled."

They were of several minds as to what to do. One

group, in which we certainly must include Alexander Hamilton, was of the opinion that here was a treasure so great that it might well be used over the years to help establish the financial credit of the new government and to pay some of its current operating expenses. Another group, perhaps one of the best spokesmen of which was Gouverneur Morris of New York, advocated the idea that this area ought to be kept perpetually in an inferior position, that it should never be on the same plane as the older communities in the Republic, that it always ought to have what you and I know so well as a colonial status.

Fortunately, neither of these ideas prevailed. A new idea current in the minds of men, which Thomas Jefferson captured and put down on paper first in 1784 in his famous Ordinance, was worked over by others and finally incorporated in the Ordinance of 1787 or the Northwest Ordinance.

I have often thought that it deserves to rank as third in the trilogy with the Declaration of Independence and the Constitution of the U.S.; for the Northwest Ordinance laid down the program of a colonial policy the like of which Europeans had never known. Its fundamental proposition was that these colonies should ultimately become the equals of the older areas. Its guiding principle was the idea that the society that went out to possess the land beyond the Appalachians must be a society trained in self-government and able to take its place within the federal union.

We have added thirty-five states to the thirteen colonies that comprised the little nation in 1776. Of these thirty-five, all but six went through the territorial stage, learned by experience the processes of self-government, and finally joined on terms of almost complete equality the older thirteen that had first formed the American Republic. They learned by experience; and in the long run they, the children, became vaster than the parent: more numerous in the Senate, more numerous in the House of Representatives, wielding an influence today, of course, which constantly dwarfs the influence of the thirteen original states along the Atlantic seaboard. A very large proportion of them—almost three fifths to be exact—came out of that great valley between the crest of the Appalachians and the peaks of the Rockies.

The American nation possessed that valley in its eastern parts at the very beginning of its independent existence. It added the western half in the early years of the nineteenth century by the Louisiana Purchase. What a valley it was! The tributaries of the Mississippi carried each year to the sea a volume of water which exceeded all the rivers of the continent of Europe, with the exception of the great Volga. Its forests of hard and soft woods stood ready for the frontiersman's axe. Under its fertile soil were deposits of coal and iron, copper and lead and oil, of which no American yet dreamed. It was a valley which in its total area almost equaled the empire that had been brought under the sway of the Emperor Trajan. Its eastern part alone, from the crest of the Appalachians to the muddy waters of the Mississippi, was as large as the area of Great Britain, the Netherlands, the German provinces, and Italy. That was the empire the young American nation was able to settle in the seventy-five years after the opening of the nineteenth century.

And Americans did it in such fortunate circumstances, for this was the period, at the end of the Napoleonic Wars, when Europe entered upon as stable a political situation internationally as she was ever to know. The Concert of Europe and later the balance-of-power managed to maintain almost for one hundred years after the Congress of Vienna a fitful peace in which these Americans worked out their destiny in the lands beyond the Appalachians. It was a period also when they themselves were moving forward with new confidence because with each passing year they felt more secure from the possibility of foreign invasion.

The Lousiana Purchase in 1803 had removed the unpredictable ambition of Napoleon Bonaparte from the American continent. The purchase of Florida in 1819 had relaxed the grasp of a feeble yet very stubborn Spain. The acquisition of Oregon had removed a large part of the fear that Britain might conceivably again move in on our northwestern approaches. The conquest of the Mexican territory and the addition of California had demonstrated to us, however reluctant we had been to fight that war, that we were militarily in no danger from the Mexicans to the southwest. And chief of all, it seems to me, the agreement arrived at between Canadians and British on the one side and Americans on the other that there should be no semblance of fortification along that great northern border—still one of the greatest borders undefended in the history of mankind—gave us assurance that we could expand with that security that has been denied through the ages to so many people all over the earth. Do I need to emphasize to this audience what a sense of national insecurity can do to the moral fiber of man?

As Americans moved into the Mississippi Valley, they had, I think, another precious heritage: the fact that for almost two centuries they had, in a way, been getting ready for the advance along the western frontiers. They knew something of what constituted the genius of their nationalism.

You and I might quarrel a little as to exactly what to include in that nationalism, but three things, I feel, we could not leave out, whatever else we might add. In the first place, by the early decades of the nineteenth century, Americans were convinced that one of the things they wanted was individual liberty. It had been a slow process to determine what they meant by that. At first, their concept of liberty had been the concept of malcontents who had left the Old World because of religious persecution, or because of political oppression, or because of economic maladjustment. At first, they had simply been libertarians in St. Paul's sense of "kicking against the pricks of fortune." But almost two hundred years on these shores had developed in them an awareness that their idea about the liberty of the individual was not merely an instrumentality to throw off restraints, monarchical or otherwise. It was an instrumentality that would lead them into the good society. It had, indeed, become a goal in itself. Perhaps no one ever said it better—though I suspect he did not even realize he was saying it—than

Thomas Jefferson in a letter to his French friend, Du Pont de Nemours, when he wrote to him about the possible consequences flowing out of the French Revolution. He said to Du Pont: "You and I both love the people. You love them as infants whom you are afraid to trust without nurses, and I love them as adults whom I freely leave to self-government." That was the difference which Thomas Jefferson thought he saw between the kind of liberty that a forward-looking Frenchman was talking about and the kind of liberty which he believed he and so many of his fellow Americans were talking about.

The second element that went into the concept of American nationalism was firm faith in the validity of the moral law. No one who reads the literature of the first fifty years of the nineteenth century can come away from that reading without saying: "Well, I may not agree with these writers, I may not completely understand what they are talking about, but they certainly had confidence that they understood the moral principles undergirding the universe." They believed in a kind of absolute distinction that could be drawn between justice and injustice, between right and wrong. That sense of moral law was compounded of a variety of things, some of which seem almost irreconcilable; and yet they were all there. It was compounded of divine revelation, as expressed in the law of the Jews as well as in the social gospel of Jesus of Nazareth. Yet it was shot through at so many points with the rationalism of the European Enlightenment. It was full of "natural right" and "natural law." The young American learned it early, for if he escaped it prior to his college years, he could not finish college and receive his baccalaureate degree without taking a course in moral philosophy, usually given by the president of the institution or by the most distinguished senior professor. In that course in moral philosophy he learned the principles of the moral law. It did not make any difference whether he came from New England or the Middle States or the South. Jefferson Davis could say with many a New Englander: "The Course I enjoyed most in my college years was the eloquence of that dear old President as he taught moral philosophy." That was the great course. We do not have it any more.

The third element in American nationalism was a confident belief in progress. Now that is nothing peculiar to Americans. Europeans believed in progress. Others in other parts of the world did also. There is nothing strange about it; but it was a sort of Americanized progress in that it carried with it the idea of mission. We were chosen! On its unlovely side, you know, it made so many European travelers talk about us as the most braggart, the most conceited, the most self-centered group in the world—the sort of comment which Professor Edman so ably presented to you at your last meeting. But, on its finer side, there was the idea that Americans had a particular mission in the world. It ran through the Election Day sermons in New England; it inspired, in spite of a lot of bombast and nationalism, so many of the 4th of July orations; it found its great expression in the poetry of Walt Whitman. In prose it has had no finer examplar than Abraham Lincoln's very simple sentence: "I have never had a feeling politically that did not spring from the *Declaration of Independence*." That it was which gave promise that the weights would be lifted in due time from the shoulders of all men and that at last all men would have an equal chance.

Do you realize that if a young man born in the United States of America at the end of the Napoleonic Wars, in shall we say 1815, as the Congress of Vienna's deliberations were beginning to remake the map of Europe, had been given a span of life of eighty-five years, he would have been able to witness most of the story of American democracy in action. His boyhood days would have been filled—and he must have heard some of the talk in his home—with the actions of state legislatures as they broadened the bases of the suffrage and removed qualifications for the right to hold office. His young manhood would have coincided with the advance of successive waves of settlers into the eastern part of the Mississippi Valley. He could have actually seen, had he been willing to travel, a frontier in which the hunter and the trapper were still the most important men, a frontier in which the pioneer farmer was girdling trees and chopping them down with his axe, and in which later the farmer with the crude plow was planting his crops beneath the bare branches of those girdled trees. He could have gone into western communities where the individual proprietor, coming with a little accumulated capital, was already beginning to build the foundation of commerce and trade and manufacture, and was providing that social soil in which it would be possible to develop the specialties of civilized life. He would have lived through the greatest travail that the American experienced, the Civil War. He would have seen the mounting protests against human bondage, whether it was indentured servants, white in skin, or enslaved Africans. He would have lived through the period when he could have said: "I know not only the farmers' frontier, but also the miners' frontier. I have seen California and Colorado brought to a great development out of the crude beginnings of migrant mine workers. I have seen the cattlemens' frontier of the Great Plains." And if he had lived, as we granted he might live, until 1900, he could have said: "I have seen this nation go from the sources of the rivers that flow eastward into the Atlantic to the waters of the blue Pacific itself. It has all been within my lifetime."

He could have said more than that. He could have said: "I know now what American democracy means. It does not mean the perfection of dogma, it does not mean a flawless systematic organization. It means taking from an older civilization the best that it had to offer, sifting it out successively on one frontier after another, and then trying haltingly, fumblingly, with many mistakes, to make it bring to us an era in which the liberty of the individual is a goal of social effort."

If he had been an honest man, he would not have said that American democracy had everywhere won victories, had everywhere been without flaw, had everywhere been above critical examination. If he had been an honest man, he would have said that America owed much to Milton and to John Locke, to Rousseau and to Montesquieu, to Grotius and to Pufendorf; that it had received untold contributions from older groups, but that all these ideas had been tested and, if not refined, at least applied in the practical experimentation of an entire nation.

If I could leave one thing with you this morning that you should remember above all other things that I have said, I would ask you to remember that the main theme of American history is this fact beyond challenge: that we in this continent of North America are a part of the whole stream of western civilization; that we are the heirs of the Greco-Roman tradition; that we are those to whom has been entrusted, along with so many others, the great heritage of Judea and the Christian faith; that we have not denied in the past and we hope we will never deny in the future those traditions and that great heritage.

≺ II ≻

THE
FOUNDING
FATHERS

AMONG *John Krout's major interests is the period of the Revolution and the founding of the nation. The national and local scenes alike have shared his attention. The three papers which follow—on Alexander Hamilton, George Washington, and the Bill of Rights—are typical of his work on this era.*

Alexander Hamilton's Place in the Founding of the Nation

This paper was delivered November 14, 1957, before the American Philosophical Society at the meetings commemorating the bicentennial of Hamilton's birth.

E V E R Y successful nation-builder of modern times— Colbert in the seventeenth century, the elder Pitt in the eighteenth, Cavour and Bismarck in the nineteenth— understood the relation of economic strength to political power, and the links between each of these and national security. Alexander Hamilton was no exception. If he seems, at times, to tower above the others in that company of talented men who brought into being the United States of America, it is because he stated more precisely and more forcefully than most of his fellows the principles which would enable his generation to use economic policy as an instrument to achieve both national unification and national power. He was not concerned primarily with the development of a consistent theory or the formulation of an ideal system. His thinking about national power was strongly conditioned by two facts: first, that the young Republic was an almost insignificant weakling in the power politics of western Europe, and second, that despite the influence of the American Revolution and the immediate impact of Adam Smith's *Wealth of Nations*, the theories and practices of mercantilism still dominated the thought and action of those who wielded political power.

It is useless to speculate on the course which Hamilton might have taken, had conditions been different; but there is fascination in reading his eloquent exposition of the international advantages of free trade which appears in the opening paragraphs of his "Report on Manufactures," submitted to the Congress in 1791. Here is no mercantilist brief, no slavish copying of British practices. It is a convincing demonstration of one of Hamilton's greatest sources of strength as a political realist—his courageous facing of the facts, however intricate, whenever he chose a plan of action.

Action, not theory, was the central theme of his entire career. There was little of the cloistered study about him. From his early years on St. Croix in the British West Indies to the hour he left Washington's Cabinet, he found himself trying to resolve increasingly complicated problems rather than to formulate logical theories. Even in little King's College, where the academic pace was much too leisurely for him, he became involved in public affairs. To be sure, he worked hard on the classics and moral philosophy; he read rapidly in Plutarch's *Lives*, Bacon's *Essays* and Hobbes's *Dialogues*, but nothing could keep him out of the momentous debate between colonies and mother country. His pen was soon active in the war of pamphlets, and so effective was his argument that he had established a reputation as one of the abler writers of his generation before the first shots were fired at Lexington and Concord.

For Hamilton the war years, in spite of his close association with Washington, were cruelly disappointing. His craving for military fame was never satisfied; yet his military service inspired, or at least did not seem to impede, his logical thinking about the problems that caught his imagination. His brilliant reports on army organization and administration, as well as his pentrating analysis of the business of raising money to fight a war, still make exciting reading. Notable as these contributions to our military annals were, they seem inconsequential compared to the essay, in the form of a letter addressed to Robert Morris, which he put into the post on the very day in 1781 that he resigned as Washington's aide.

This message to Morris, newly established in his position as Superintendent of Finances, looms larger the longer one contemplates it. Here Hamilton, just past his twenty-fourth birthday (or his twenty-sixth, if one accepts the most recent calculations of historical scholars), boldly stated the principles essential for the building of a strong nation. Some of his associates had heard his thesis in fragmentary form on other occasions; but he had never indicated so explicitly how he would use political power, if it ever came to him. His plan was much too bold for Morris, who was naturally cautious, in spite of his financial speculations, and at the moment uncertain of his own ability to lead. The Financier could not know that his young correspondent had actually provided him with a workable blueprint for the next decade—and for generations thereafter.

But nothing that Hamilton wrote in later years reveals

any more clearly the shape of a nation in the making. Out of his awareness of local prejudices, provincial rivalries, and the clamor for state sovereignty came his insistence that the Republic, to which he was emotionally devoted, must begin to "think continentally." Out of his contempt for the vague and the visionary, he fashioned a plan that was difficult but possible, bold but not dangerous, furthering the self-interest of men of property but cleverly contrived to use that self-interest for the public good. He did not fall into the error of so many in his generation, who persisted in confusing the economy of the private household with the principles of public finance.

What the nation needed most, Hamilton argued, was a currency adequate to its business needs and financial credit sound enough to command international confidence. Both could be provided by a national bank under public auspices, but attractive to private capital. Such an institution would

create a mass of credit that will supply the defect of moneyed capital, and answer all the purposes of cash; a plan which will offer adventurers immediate advantages, analogous to those they receive by employing their money in trade, and eventually greater advantages; a plan which will give them the greatest security the nature of the case will admit for what they lend; and which will not only advance their own and secure the independence of their country, but, in its progress, have the most beneficial influence upon its future commerce, and be a source of national wealth and strength.

Hamilton admitted that the "national wealth and strength" would be dependent upon the willingness of the government to borrow against its future and to pledge complete repayment of all its debts. He quickly tried to quiet the opposition of those who feared such a burden by characterizing a national debt as "a national blessing." "It will be a powerful cement of our union. It will also create a necessity for keeping up taxation to a degree, which, without being oppressive, will be a spur to industry." Probably no part of Hamilton's plan came closer to the English model, which he so greatly admired, and certainly no other feature was so violently attacked.

The financial proposals in the 1781 memorandum were less startling than the frank revelation of his political nationalism. On this theme his words were never to be "sicklied o'er" with moderation. The weaknesses of the Continental Congress, the lack of a strong central government, could not be corrected by the Articles of Confederation, which had just been ratified. A century and three-quarters after the event, one cannot read his words without being convinced of the genuineness of his alarm. "Disastrous dissolution" would be the fate of the Republic at its very beginning unless Congress was given "complete sovereignty in all but the mere municipal law of each state." "I wish to see a convention of all the States, with full power to alter and amend, finally and irrevocably, the *present futile and senseless Confederation*." It is no exaggeration to regard this as the "first call" for the Constitutional Convention which finally met in May, 1787.

Almost forty years ago Henry Jones Ford insisted that the events of 1787 constituted for the young New Yorker his "wonderful year." And so it was. This was the time when Hamilton began to build on the blueprint of 1781. He had help in construction, but there is a large measure of truth in the assertion of some historians that we owe to Hamilton more than to any other person the fact that we have a federal constitution and that we are a union rather than a league of jealous and warring states. His was the determination, the fixed objective, the steady hand. Much has been made of his relatively minor role in the Philadelphia Convention, his dislike of both the New Jersey and the Virginia plans and his own futile proposal of a plan of government as close to the "English model as circumstances and the temper of the people would permit." "I have no scruple," he declared, "that the British government is the best in the world and I doubt much whether anything short of it will do in America."

Such a sentiment, set against the silence with which the Convention treated his proposals, and his speedy departure for New York, seems to mark his complete failure at Philadelphia. But this is a superficial view. It was Hamilton, neither Washington nor Madison nor Jay nor Franklin, who had made the Constitutional Convention possible. He had moved from the feeble conference of Virginia and Maryland commissioners at Mount Vernon in 1785 to the unsuccessful convention a year later at Annapolis, attended by representatives of only five states. But with Madison's help he used failure at Annapolis as the sounding board against which to issue the call for a meeting in 1787 that was successful. Hamilton's departure from Philadelphia was not the act of a leader too stubborn to compromise, who sulks at the first rebuff. So it has been portrayed by some of his biographers; but they are mistaken. He used the weeks from June 30 until September 2, when he returned to Philadelphia, in trying to overcome hostility to the whole idea underlying the Convention and in preparing men's minds for whatever compromise the delegates might finally approve.

His persuasive efforts involved no speeches, no appearances before mass meetings, no appeals to the crowd. Hamilton's medium was the written word. As a political essayist, he was unsurpassed. His articles appeared in the press, his encouraging letters went to Washington and Rufus King in the Convention, to Jeremiah Wadsworth, David Humphreys, and other friends in New England, advising them how to answer the Convention's foes. It was a period of preparation for the defense of the Constitution that was to come. Indeed, some of the letters of this period may have been as influential as some of the essays that comprise *The Federalist*.

Anyone who reads widely in the incomparable *Federalist* essays, in which Madison and Jay joined Hamilton, will quickly realize what Thomas Jefferson meant when he said "in some parts it is discoverable that the author means only to say what may be best said in defense of opinions in which he did not concur." He could not have come closer to the mark, if he had known that he was really aiming at Hamilton, for the young New Yorker never tried to conceal his disagreement with many of the provisions of the Constitution—though he gladly signed it. It was the measure of his statesmanship—that he put his own opinions aside, overcame his personal prejudices, and accepted the document as the only safeguard against "disunion and anarchy." Having made that decision, he never wavered in his public support of the work of the Convention. He wrote the major portion of the *Federalist* essays, which Jefferson praised as "the best commentary on the principles of government which ever was written"; and no American voice has ever dissented from that appraisal.

Hamilton's contemporaries, as well as his biographers, have been in substantial agreement that his own effort was the deciding factor in persuading New York to ratify the proposed Constitution at the Poughkeepsie Convention in 1788. When the document became fundamental law the following year, his most important work was actually finished. He had made his great gift to his fellow countrymen. He had shown them how their slender resources might be marshaled effectively to provide the national defense and domestic tranquility which they so sorely needed. His whole fiscal and financial program, as Secretary of the Treasury, had been explicitly stated years before he entered Washington's cabinet. However remarkable the famous Reports of 1790 and 1791, they rest securely on political foundation stones which Hamilton had set a decade earlier: first, the business and propertied classes generally must be tied by bonds of self-interest to the national government; and second, public policy should be directed toward the encouragement of economic diversification—including manufacturing and commerce as well as agriculture— capable of creating an integrated national economy and a firm political union.

The translation of his policies into law was a major

triumph for the Secretary of the Treasury, but it was less important for the young Republic than the imaginative formulation of the principles out of which the policies grew. Indeed, the years during which Congress accepted the financial program known as the "Hamiltonian System" were marred by the blunders of the man who had written the legislation. Hamilton was not content to serve merely as a Chancellor of the Exchequer. He never overcame his desire to be regarded as the Prime Minister. He gave Washington advice, even when the President had not requested it, on foreign policy, legal affairs, military problems, and matters of protocol. In the process he established precedents which are still followed, but he also alienated associates in the government whose support would have been invaluable.

Perhaps Hamilton's greatest weakness in the half dozen years of the apparent triumph of his fiscal and economic policies was his failure to understand how rapidly the political opinions of his fellow countrymen were changing. Between the inauguration of George Washington and the election of Thomas Jefferson in 1800 a process of education in democracy had been going forward steadily. Wherever Hamilton encountered this process, he was inclined either to oppose or to ignore it. He refused to see that the Jeffersonian doctrine of "the cherishment of the people" encouraged the greatest possible diffusion of political power among a progressively educated body of citizens. Instead, he regarded the Republicans, who carefully nurtured the Jeffersonian doctrine, as a group of fractional insurgents, too quick in their imitation of the French Jacobins. But the Republicans had sensed the temper of this generation. To their standard rather than to the symbols of the Federalist party, the new voters were drawn. As a result, Hamilton and his associates were able only to design and construct the new edifice of government; men motivated by a broader concept of their civic responsibility moved in and took over the completed structure.

They did not dare, however, to destroy Hamilton's design. Indeed, they modified but slightly the precedents which he had set. Federalist institutions, even Federalist policies, survived, surprisingly intact. The Bank and the public funds remained undisturbed. The military and naval establishments, though reduced in size, were not abolished. The hated excise tax was repealed and other internal revenue duties were modified; but the Republicans in Congress initiated no general assault on the powers of the central government, which Hamilton had done so much to create.

Many Americans today are inclined to regard the first Secretary of the Treasury as merely an adroit politician, brilliant and versatile, but no greater in his influence on later generations that the short-lived Federalist party to which he belonged. A partisan leader he was, and a determined one. Yet no strategy of his in the political arena, not even his triumph in persuading the First Congress to accept his fiscal plans, can compare with the persistent force of his economic ideas. His critics, as well as his friends, recognized that during his years of service in Washington's cabinet he seemed to do the thinking for the administration.

The leaven of Hamilton's thought in time brought

action even within the ranks of the Jeffersonian Republicans. By 1815 the leaders of the faction, dubbed the
"War Hawks," had accepted a nationalistic program
highly imitative of the "Hamiltonian System." Though
they had won no decisive victory over the British during
the War of 1812, they had captured President Madison
and persuaded him to accept their program. It was, therefore, James Madison, once Thomas Jefferson's chief lieu-
tenant, who wrote the proposals of the economic nationalists into his presidential message of December, 1815.
Josiah Quincy, Massachusetts Federalist, listening to that
message, sarcastically remarked that the Republican party
had "out-Federalized Federalism"; for Madison asked the
Congress to approve (1) a liberal provision for national
defense, (2) governmental aid for the construction of
roads and canals, (3) encouragement to manufacturers by
means of a protective tariff, and (4) the re-establishment
of a National Bank. Though the words were Madison's,
many in both House and Senate must have been thinking
of Alexander Hamilton.

The response of the Congress was quick and enthusiastic. A committee of the House, headed by John C.
Calhoun, reported a bill to establish a Bank of the United
States, not unlike the First Bank which had ceased to
exist with the expiration of its Charter in 1811. A few of
the "Old Republicans," like John Taylor of Virginia,
protested against this "surrender to the money power,"
but most of their Republican colleagues accepted the
Bank as a necessary extension of the powers of the national government. Henry Clay, with a characteristically
dramatic flourish, rose to confess that he had spoken

vigorously against the recharter of the old Bank in 1811, but that he was now sacrificing consistency for the welfare of his country. The sense of high drama must have been heightened for those among his hearers who realized that his eloquent speech closely followed Hamilton's arguments in 1791, when he wrote for Washington a defense of the constitutionality of the first Bank bill.

Nor was Henry Clay the only leader in his generation who turned to the writings of Hamilton for inspiration, even for the effective phrasing of ideas. John Marshall, then brilliantly engaged in reenforcing the spirit of nationalism, presided over a Supreme Court that handed down a series of opinions calculated to strengthen the federal government and to give judicial sanction to the doctrine of the implied powers to be derived from the Constitution. Few decisions have had greater influence on the course of constitutional government in this country than Marshall's opinion in the case of *McCulloch vs. Maryland* in 1819. His vigorous argument, upholding the power of Congress to charter a bank, was actually a rephrasing, in somewhat more legalistic terms, of Hamilton's classic exposition of the doctrine of implied powers.

Though sectional rivalries and partisan politics thwarted the plans of these economic nationalists early in the nineteenth century, their followers in a later generation carried similar views into the Republican party. Young Abraham Lincoln in Illinois, a devoted supporter of Henry Clay and the American System, was but one of many whose imagination was quickened by the spirit of nationalism that pervades every public paper written by Alexander Hamilton. Consider, for example, Lincoln's first political speech. The report of it may be apocryphal; yet the tone is so characteristic of him that it almost compels acceptance. In announcing his candidacy for the Illinois state legislature early in 1832, he said:

I presume you all know who I am. I am humble Abraham Lincoln. I have been solicited by many friends to become a candidate for the Legislature. My politics are short, and sweet, like the old woman's dance. I am in favor of a national bank. I am in favor of the internal improvement system, and a high protective tariff. These are my sentiments and political principles. If elected, I shall be thankful; if not, it will be all the same.

Though the personal mood is alien to Hamilton, the political program is his.

Surely it is not merely the eye of fancy that sees in the Congressional legislation of the Civil War years some of the greatest triumphs of the Hamiltonian philosophy. His ideas were but slightly modified by those who championed such laws as the protective tariffs of 1862 and 1864, the granting of federal lands to the Union Pacific and Central Pacific railroads, the establishment of a national banking system in 1863, and the passage of a contract labor law to stimulate European immigration. Every one of these measures received the approval of the Illinois "railsplitter" in the White House, who had dedicated his life to the preservation of the Union which Hamilton had done so much to build.

It is wise for us to remember that Hamilton, like every worthy statesman, spoke and wrote in context. His United States of America was a young and relatively insignificant republic in the great family of nations. His task was to give it energetic leadership in the uncertain years of its infancy. His loyalty transcended every parochialism and embraced the nation. His quest was for national strength, and he used skillfully whatever resources promised to be most effective. Among the founders of this nation none argued more eloquently than he for that combination of private enterprise and governmental policies which has made industrial America what it is today. And none succeeded so well in translating theory into action.

Reprinted with permission from the American Philosophical Society's PROCEEDINGS, *102:124–28, April, 1958.*

Washington
as a Nation Builder

This address was delivered before the Washington Association of New Jersey at Washington's Headquarters, Morristown, N.J., February 20, 1960.

I T would be an exciting thing for anyone to stand on this historic ground and think with you about the years of the first President of the United States. In 1889 when Edwin Booth made that royal gift to his fellow actors which came to be known as The Players, he pointed out to them that he wished they would make provision in the clubhouse at sixteen Gramercy Park for the very considerable collection of portraits of actors which he had brought together over the years. This they agreed to do, but Mr. Booth had one portrait which he greatly prized but about which he was hesitant. It was a portrait of George Washington, and he confided to one of his friends in The Players he had misgivings about the appropriateness of having Washington's portrait alongside the portraits of these men who had achieved fame in the American and English theatre.

Lawrence Barrett, his friend, said to him, "Think nothing more about it. What could be more appropriate than for George Washington to be put alongside these actors. After all, wasn't he our leading man?" That quip contains essential truth and it constitutes really the theme that I would like to discuss with you.

Washington, in a generation that produced an extraordinary number of distinguished political leaders, towered above all of his contemporaries. He did not have the unusual brilliance of Alexander Hamilton; he lacked the painstaking scholarship of James Madison; he didn't possess the encyclopedic knowledge and interests of Benjamin Franklin; he certainly had not the inventive genius of Thomas Jefferson; and yet there wasn't one of his associates who so completely brought together the traits which would make it possible to establish a nation.

The various qualities that made him the leader among the galaxy of his fellows are a little difficult for us to grasp at the present time, I suspect in large part because of the fact that Washington to our generation comes through in a sort of monolithic way. He seems to be so aloof from things that are warmly human, so distant even in the days of his own career from the intimate anecdotes that surround a large number of the persons who participated in the founding of the nation.

There was a rather austere dignity about him, which was not completely misrepresented in Stuart's Athenæum portrait. There was also a feeling by those who were most closely associated with him that there were certain reserves that you just did not dare to break through so far as the Virginia gentleman was concerned. And yet I think, if we stop to analyze carefully, there are a number of traits that emerged very quickly as indicating some of the reasons why Washington was the leading man in the drama of his whole generation.

First of those, if I were to judge, would be the characteristic of fortitude, by which I mean a happy combination of courage and patience. No one ever doubted during his whole lifetime the physical bravery of George Washington. And as the war went on, those who saw him in military service increased the number of reports of things that they had witnessed that showed his complete disdain for anything that savored of concern about his physical safety.

One Continental soldier waxed eloquent over the fact that he had witnessed Washington on the ramparts of Fort Putnam training his field glasses on the combat that was going on below him, at a time when he could easily have been within the range of the cross fire of the combatants. Said this Continental, for the first time he began to sense the fact that he didn't have to duck every time he heard the rattle of musketry, that he could, like his Commander-in-Chief, ignore some of the considerations of safety.

But physical courage was just a small part of the fortitude that made the man great. It was the infinite patience he combined with it, the ability to handle without indicating too frequently his irritations. Though how he could indicate being irritated when he wanted to! But the patience is magnified by the fact that we know he had an inherent capacity for righteous indignation that was tremendous when he let it explode. But most of the time he could put up with the sort of thing that he had to endure from some of his close associates in the Continental Army; with the kind of disloyalty that Charles Lee on more than one occasion revealed; with the constant grumbling of as good a leader as General Sullivan, always complaining about everything that went on that didn't suit him; with the tremendous incompetence of a man like General Heath; with the envious desire for power that seemed to motivate Horatio Gates much more often than it should; with the incessant demands of the various European military leaders after they got here that they be given proper rank and proper position in any kind of military operation that Washington might be planning.

To have endured all that was certainly trouble enough for the most patient soul, and yet remember that that was superficial compared to the fact that he, who knew so well the importance of a well-ruled, well-trained, well-provisioned army, had to deal with a group that frequently came to the point of degenerating into bands of guerilla operators.

That they never quite did that, it seems to me, we can credit almost exclusively to the fortitude of the Commander-in-Chief—an army that was rarely paid, that was usually poorly clad, that was constantly hungry, and hungry in a land that was reveling in plenty during much of this time. When civilians had enough to eat, the army was starving. Yet Washington was able to hold that group together, and with a very few exceptions, to prevent it from pillaging the countryside, foraging for food, and getting out of hand, in its demands for adequate pay, proper clothing, and decent sustenance.

The second characteristic which he unquestionably demonstrated throughout his years, not only in the war but afterward, was his determination—his determination to get to the goal, no matter how great the obstacles were. He never swerved from his demand that the whole effort of everyone be directed toward the creation of an independent nation in which the military power would be forever subject to the civil authority. Is there any better illustration of that determination than that thrilling episode at Newburgh when an army that had long gone without pay, bitterly resentful of what it thought was the hopeless incompetence of the Continental Congress, reached the point where it felt, in the words of Major Armstrong, that there was no recourse for the Commander-in-Chief but to declare himself a military dictator, march on Congress, take power into his own hands, and if necessary become a monarch in the newly independent United States of America.

That episode is passed so often in a tiny footnote in history books, or with a brief paragraph that doesn't attempt to go into the amazing test of character that Washington endured at Newburgh when he stopped that revolt of his own officers and men and persuaded them that the thing to do was to send an additional petition to Congress. And how many petitions they had sent in the years before, that had either been ignored or produced no tangible results!

And yet you remember that he managed to play the part with a dramatic forthrightness that moved many who saw it to tears. As he sat down to sign the paper that would urge the officers and men to follow his advice rather than to resort to violence, he asked those gathered around the desk whether they would forgive him if he would put on his spectacles, because he said, "As my hair has grown gray, so I have become almost blind in the service of my country."

And yet that service to him, he was determined, should end in only one way: the creation of a republican form of government with the subjection of the military to the civil authority in the newly formed United States.

A third trait was his humility, the selflessness with which he carried himself during the years of the war and afterwards. Did ever a man who had received the highest prize of his fellow citizens more clearly show that he hadn't the slightest desire for their accolades, that there was nothing in his makeup that wanted praise, consideration of his personal estate, honor for what he was doing in the name of the young and untested nation.

He had that quality that I think probably no one expressed better than Sir Isaac Newton did earlier in the eighteenth century when he wrote in the closing years of his life: "I know not what the world will say about my work, but to me it has always seemed that I was much as a child playing along the seashore, now and then finding a prettier pebble or a more beautiful shell than my companions, while before me lay the whole ocean of truth, undiscovered."

Isn't that spirit the beginning of wisdom? And it's the selflessness that you find in Washington at every point that you probe into his career. He was always a man of the greatest prudence. You often use that word to mean a person who is just a little timorous, afraid of the unknown, unwilling to venture. Well, do you think there is any of that in a man who would leave that wonderful estate at Mount Vernon and risk everything he had in this world—property, possessions, position, prestige, friends—in a cause which he hadn't the remotest idea could succeed. There is no prudence there, except the prudence of a wise man who understands how to reconcile dreams of the future with the realities of history.

We have seen in the course of our national existence a great many men and women who have dreamed dreams. And sometimes they have been magnificent dreams, and often we have watched those dreams turn out in the end to be veritable nightmares, because those who had them lacked that attribute of prudence which helped them to realize that dreams, no matter how noble, have got to be reconciled with the realities of history.

When Jefferson finally left the Cabinet, disgusted probably with what he thought were Hamilton's unnecessary maneuverings, he remarked that the attribute of the President which most impressed him was his prudence. He may have said it in a slightly sneering fashion, being at the moment not too favorably impressed by George Washington, but however he meant it, he spoke the truth. One of Washington's greatest characteristics was prudence, and an imprudent man could not have done everything that was done in the Revolutionary period, could have lost not only the battles but have lost the war and failed to reach his objective. Washington lost plenty of battles. In many respects he was not a superior military leader, but he had the thing that went far beyond anything in the field of tactics or strategy, was the embodiment of the best there was in the American people in his generation. And that made him wisely prudent in every decision that he had to reach.

It's quite a common practice for modern historians to make a great deal of the fact that Washington leaned very heavily upon his associates; in the war upon some of the younger officers in headquarters; in a later period upon the members of his Cabinet, notably Alexander Hamilton.

Having only a few years ago gone through the celebration of the two hundredth anniversary of Alexander Hamilton, may I comment that I'm not convinced that it was Hamilton leading Washington. I suspect there was a remarkable cooperation, but I also suspect that George Washington reached the decisions after consultation to be sure, especially on economic and financial matters, with as brilliant a mind as Hamilton's unquestionably was, and using the advice he got in a way which so few of us are willing to use advice.

I need not remind you that we all have a habit in a time of crisis of turning to close friends or professional persons whom we think can advise us, listening to what they have to say, and then going away and doing exactly as we please, paying no attention to the advice we have received.

That wasn't the way of the first President of the United States. He listened; he weighed it carefully. He didn't necessarily fall under the spell of Hamilton or any other person, but his decision was founded upon the facts which he felt he had gathered. And think what he had to do as the creator of a government under the

Constitution. He with his associates established the cabinet system, unknown to the Constitution, and not really to this day embodied in statute law, except as the statutes create certain departments of administration.

He it was who fixed the cabinet system. Some of you may be saying, "Oh, it would never have been fixed if it hadn't been for Hamilton." But remember this, that a quarrel between Hamilton and Jefferson came as near to wrecking the possibility of a cabinet system as anything that you can imagine. And if it hadn't been for a prudent man in the presidency, you never would have had the cabinet system created, put into operation as a fundamental part of the government of the United States.

Here was a nation starting out at a time when the world generally regarded it with distaste, if not with positive alarm. We sometimes forget that the United States was regarded as a dangerous experiment when it was begun. It would have been so easy to say, as some of his cabinet advisers at one time or other wanted him to say: We can't go along alone. We either must have British help or we must have French help, or we must have the help of others who can assist us in combating both English and French.

That never was Washington's way. He it was who salvaged something out of the unfortunate Jay's treaty. He it was who made sure that the advantages of Pinckney's treaty were to be fully realized in the end. He it was who in those first eight terrible years made sure that the United States of America was not swallowed up in Europe's wars.

It isn't easy, I grant you, to see some of these attributes

when you think of the rather distant, remote personality, but if you will get behind the Stuart portraits, if you will avoid the stereotype that fills so many of our minds of the unapproachable military leader and statesman, you will see, I think, the qualities of human strength and human weakness that enabled us to have in this period a leading man who stayed with the drama to a happy conclusion.

Reprinted with permission of the Washington Association of New Jersey.

The American
Bill of Rights

F E W aspects of the Constitution of the United States aroused more unfavorable comment during the historic debates over ratification than the fact that the document contained no "bill of rights." The American people, out of their experience as colonials, quite as much as from their reading of political theory, had become convinced that there were certain inalienable rights possessed by the individual, which no government, whatever its popular majority, had the power to infringe. This conviction had been happily stated in Jefferson's famous phrases in the Declaration of Independence. Both the idea and the phrasing were in large measure derived from the English Declaration of Right, the Bill of Rights, and the political theories of "the great Mr. Locke." Yet the American revolutionists realized that they were confronted by conditions not easily described in terms of earlier theory or practice. The "Glorious Revolution" had demonstrated the power of Parliament to protect the individual against the Crown, but it had erected very few signposts to mark the way for a people determined to pursue happiness as they pleased. The proper rules for that pursuit would have to be of their own making.

Their inclination to separate alienable from inalienable human rights seemed to flow logically from their belief in the law of nature, independent of the state and its laws. Theophilus Parsons in *The Essex Result* (1778) had succinctly stated the nature of the difference. There were some rights which could be voluntarily entrusted by a people to its government, but other rights which could not be surrendered even to a government based upon the consent of the governed. Among the political leaders who framed the American Constitution there was apparent agreement that the concept of inalienable rights needed more precise definition, but only a few advocated an attempt to write into the fundamental law an explanation of what was meant by "Life, Liberty and the pursuit of Happiness." Indeed, the deliberations of the Constitutional Convention in 1787 had almost reached a close before Elbridge Gerry of Massachusetts, prompted by George Mason of Virginia, moved that a bill of rights be drafted. Mason, who had prepared the Virginia Bill of Rights which served as a model for other states, insisted that an enumeration of fundamental liberties was as necessary in the federal constitution as in the state constitutions; but most of his colleagues did not agree. Not one of the state delegations supported Gerry's motion. Probably many of them were persuaded by the argument of Roger Sherman of Connecticut that the state declarations of rights were sufficient to guarantee fundamental liberties, regardless of what was written into the new instrument of federal government.

But the omission of a bill of rights came quickly under the scrutiny of the state ratifying conventions. In Massachusetts, for example, the delegates were amazed, just as George Mason had predicted, that the document contained no guarantee of trial by jury in civil cases. The spirited argument over that point finally compelled the Federalist leaders to admit that ratification could probably not be secured unless the delegates endorsed certain amendments "to remove the fears and quiet the apprehensions of many of the good people" of the Commonwealth. By a clever device the resolution of ratification became also a demand for subsequent amendment. On nine specific points Massachusetts made suggestions which would either limit the powers of Congress or modify the procedures in the federal courts. Thus waverers were brought into line for ratification, and a pattern was set which won support for the Constitution in other states.

Seven of the thirteen states went on record as favoring some form of declaration concerning popular rights. Their proposals ranged from specific changes in the structure and powers of the various agencies of government to rather lengthy statements of the basic principles on which all governments should be based. Implicit in all of them, however, was the desire for protection of individual liberties against an abuse of power by the state. Without these proposals for a bill of rights, the Constitution probably would not have been ratified in 1788. In addition, they constituted a sort of "moral obligation" which the new federal government promptly accepted.

The First Congress under the Constitution gave serious consideration to more than 120 proposed amendments and accepted twelve of them. By December 15, 1791, ten, having been duly ratified by the states, became the bill of rights. Among the proposals which the Congress failed to approve, however, was one that James Madison regarded as a cogent and comprehensive expression of popular opinion, an appropriate preamble to the more specific amendments. It would have served, he believed, as a power line between the political theory of the Declaration of Independence and the structure of government set forth in the Constitution. None could then have been in doubt concerning the purpose for which the constitutional machinery had been created. "All power," the framers of that rejected resolution insisted, "is originally vested in and consequently derived from the people. . . . Government is instituted and ought to be exercised for the benefit of the people; which consists in the enjoyment of life and liberty, with the right of acquiring and using property and generally of pursuing and obtaining happiness and safety. There are certain natural rights of which men, when they form a social compact, cannot deprive or divest their posterity, among which are the enjoyment of life and liberty."

Here, then, is the spirit in which the American Bill of Rights was formulated. It is sustained in large part by those individualistic notions of the social contract which persisted from Hobbes, through Locke to Rousseau, but it is also sensitive to Rousseau's concept of a "common good" transcending the separate interests of individuals. It recognizes that a community of interest may come from a mingling of individual differences, but only if man is free to transmit to his fellows something of the intellectual harvests which come from the cultivation of his own inalienable rights. Basic is the conviction that respect for the reason and conscience of the individual man will increase the power of reason in the universe, and thus give greater assurance that human affairs will be dominated by reasonable men. This it was which Benjamin Franklin understood when he wrote: "Without freedom of thought there can be no such thing as wisdom, and no such thing as public liberty without freedom of speech."

There was doubt among the founders of the Republic whether the cause of government based upon the consent of the governed would be forwarded by a mere enumeration of the liberties of individual men. Such inalienable rights, John Dickinson argued, "must be preserved by soundness of sense and honesty of heart. Compared with these what are a bill of rights, or any characters drawn upon paper or parchment?" But once it was decided that a list of individual rights should be attempted, there was little dispute concerning the primary sources. Ready to hand were the declarations of rights prepared by various state legislatures and the codifications which had gone into most of the newly written state constitutions. Even more pertinent, however, was British political folklore—Magna Carta, the common law guarantees of civil liberty, the Petition of Right, the Bill of Rights, and a multitude of popular myths which had been originally derived from these historic documents. Some articles in the first ten amendments to the American Constitution are almost literally transcribed from the English Bill of Rights, while phrase after phrase calls to mind George Mason and the Virginia pronouncements.

Yet one can be too easily misled by these verbal similarities. The federal Bill of Rights avoids the excursions into political philosophy which distinctively marked many of the earlier state declarations. Its parallelism at certain points with the English Bill of Rights—and this is not mere unimaginative imitation—tends to obscure the fact that the two documents rest upon somewhat different assumptions. Both, to be sure, are concerned with specific potential threats to human liberty and with the practical means of thwarting them. For the English, however, the source of danger was the unrestrained prerogative of the Crown, and the defense was sought in the power exercised by a majority in the Parliament. For Americans, the danger seemed to lie in the will of the majority, as expressed through its representatives in Congress assembled. The defense was therefore more complicated.

That is why the American Bill of Rights is so often presented as an exercise in constitutional negativism. Its provisions are arbitrarily classified as of two sorts: those which impose substantive restrictions upon Congress and those which list procedural compulsions designed to protect individual liberties. Some commentators have gone so far as to interpret the effect of the first ten amendments almost exclusively in terms of our fear of a democratically motivated government. They have emphasized, often unduly, the hostility to majority rule which seems to be inherent in the attempt to protect minority rights; the distrust of the elected representatives of the people which is apparent in prohibitions imposed on Congress; the danger that a government severely limited in the name of individual liberties may finally be rendered ineffectual in meeting insistent social problems.

Such commentaries—and they have not been infrequent during the past quarter century—are the result either of a curious misunderstanding or a deliberate misinterpretation. Let us take the First Amendment to the Constitution: "Congress shall make no law respecting an establishment of religion, or prohibiting the free exercise thereof, or abridging the freedom of speech, or of the press; or the right of the people peaceably to assemble, and to petition the government for a redress of grievances." Here are definite actions which the Congress is forbidden to take. By whom? As a representative of the will of the majority, it wields the greatest political power possible in a democracy. If it is estopped from exercising that power, then the obstruction must come from a minority. And so it does, but it comes from a minority only because the community has enumerated certain individual rights which may not be infringed by government. "The community," so Professor R. M. MacIver in *The Web of Government* aptly puts it, "has gone on record that it will not suffer the state to regulate these dispositions. The community that vests government with powers reserves certain rights against these powers, in this respect limits the power of the state. In this sense a democratic state is always a limited state."

But it does not follow, as some would have us believe, that a limited state is a weak state, on the road toward ultimate impotence. The very rights which the First Amendment, for example, hedges against government are calculated to make the community strong. For social strength depends upon the right of the individual to think his own thoughts, to communicate his reasoned opinions to others, to discuss with his fellows the ideas and aspirations which he has in common with them. Unless this primary area of liberty is maintained against arbitrary governmental interference, man can have no sense of freedom from oppression in his home, his school, or his church. If it is properly defended in a democratic state, then the minority and the majority are free to search for those policies which will best contribute to the harmonizing of their diverse or conflicting interests.

The Bill of Rights means not only restriction on government but also opportunity for the citizen. That opportunity is really antecedent to the democratic process itself. It gives the citizen freedom to work toward the conversion of minority opinion into majority opinion; or to hold up decisions, based upon transient majorities, until reasonable arguments can exert their influence over a longer period of time. It gives him a sense of belonging to the community, even if his vote does not fall on the side of governmental policy. More certainly than any other device known to democracy, it guarantees thoughtful consideration for all controversial questions.

Lest this seem to be just another way of saying that the minority is always right, or that minority rights are forever at the mercy of the "tyranny of the majority," it should be emphasized that limitations on the authority of government can be a most salutary influence both in determining and in executing the popular will. Out of the Bill of Rights has come much political education for the people of the United States. Thomas Jefferson argued that such would be the case, when he urged Madison in 1789 to make sure that the Constitution was amended to safeguard individual liberties. "In the arguments in favor of a declaration of rights," he wrote, "you omit one which has great weight with me; the legal check which it puts into the hands of the judiciary. This is a body which rendered independent and kept strictly to its own department, merits great confidence for its learning and integrity." Though Jefferson's faith in the wisdom of judges, or at least in their good sense in staying within their proper jurisdiction, soon disappeared, he never faltered in his belief that the constant discussion of fundamental freedoms and the perennial effort to define essential human rights would go far toward educating the people in the meaning of democracy. His First Inaugural Address reminded his hearers of their obligations as citizens: "All too, will bear in mind this sacred principle, that though the will of the majority is in all cases to prevail, that will to be rightful must be reasonable; that the minority possess their equal rights which law must protect, and to violate would be oppression." So stated, the problem of minority rights and majority will becomes really a prolonged process of education in political democracy.

Throughout our history one of the chief educational values of the federal Bill of Rights has been the fact that it is a constant reminder that rights cannot be separated from responsibilities. This must have been in the minds of the Connecticut leaders in 1818, when they finally replaced the old royal charter with a new constitution. Their bill of rights contained this statement: "Every citizen may freely speak, write, and publish his sentiments on all subjects, being responsible for the abuse of that liberty." The conjunction of "right" and "responsibility" is here unmistakable, and it is symbolic of an attitude which has permeated our thinking about democracy, determined the formulation of our laws, and influenced the decisions of our courts. And the conjunction over the years has been salutary. No one has ever stated the case more persuasively than did Carl L. Becker in his *Freedom and Responsibility in the American Way of Life.* "Freedom unrestrained by responsibility," he wrote, "becomes mere license; responsibility unchecked by freedom becomes mere arbitrary power. The question, then, is not whether freedom and responsibility shall be united, but how they can be united and reconciled to the best advantage . . . the difficulty being to reconcile the desirable liberties of the individual with the necessary power of government in such a way as to do justice as well as may be to the desires and interests of all individuals and classes in society."

Those who were anxious to resolve this difficulty have relied at times, as Jefferson anticipated they would, upon the "learning and integrity" of the judiciary. But there are variant opinions concerning the results of such reliance. It is the contention of Professor Henry S. Commager, whose sharply incisive argument may be read in his *Majority Rule and Minority Rights*, that if we "grant the desirability or necessity of calling in the judiciary to protect civil liberties" then we "concede that the majority is not to be trusted in what is perhaps the most important field of legislative activity." And he adds:

"The tendency to decide issues of personal liberty in the judicial arena alone has the effect of dulling the people into apathy towards issues that are fundamentally their concern, with the comforting notion that the courts will take care of personal and minority rights." One may sympathize with this point of view, and still not be convinced that "majority will does not imperil minority rights, either in theory or in operation." It is probably true that many apparent attacks upon freedom of speech or the press, upon religious liberty, upon the right of assembly, are not clearcut violations of the federal Bill of Rights, and therefore cannot be satisfactorily dealt with through judicial review of legislation. It may also be true that much of the legislation which seems to infringe upon personal liberties is inspired "not by hostility to those rights but—generally—by a sincere but misguided desire to preserve them." If confusion, rather than malice, is the motivation of such attacks, then we would be wise to meet them through "discussion and education, not coercion." Yet timing—and particularly a long period of time—is essential for such strategy. The appeal to the courts, which is implicit in the First Amendment to the Constitution, may be the first line of defense in the long fight for individual freedom. To place complete reliance in the legislative majority on every occasion may be more valorous than wise.

There are many who see resort to the courts in civil liberties cases in a different perspective. They are inclined to make a distinction between the will of the legislative majority, when it deals with current economic and social problems, and that same will when it undertakes to invade those imprescriptible rights which are set forth in the first ten amendments. The differentiation may be an inconsistent one—and indeed it has been so labeled—but it illumines what was said earlier in this paper about the Bill of Rights as an educational process. If the decisions of our lawmakers—municipal, state, and federal—are to be truly in accord with the "consent of the governed," there can be no curbs upon freedom of thought and no barriers against the easy communication of ideas. To protect the processes of democratic action, even by the fiat of judicial review, is not so much to restrict the will of the majority as to make that will more responsive to the opinions of free men.

If there are some who fear that such doctrine will merely make free speech a refuge for the knave and finally convert liberty into license, they should be reminded that the concept of "clear and present danger," first suggested by Justice Holmes, still stands as the test whenever the latitude of the freedoms specified in the Bill of Rights is questioned. Within the past decade, as Professor Vincent Barnett remarked, the Court "has made of it the chief touchstone in the judgment of cases involving civil liberties." So long as this is true there is little danger that we shall be compelled, as Carl L. Becker phrased it, to protect "the principle of free speech to the point where writhing in pain among its worshipers it commits suicide." There likewise seems to be little danger that the present reach of judicial protection of civil liberties will be materially reduced.

It is appropriate, nevertheless, to close this paper with a repetition of the warning that our fundamental freedoms cannot be guaranteed solely by enumeration in fundamental law or by the decisions of learned justices. Responsibility of the informed citizen must still match the inalienable rights which he desires to enjoy. The American Bill of Rights performs its noblest function, as it increases that sense of duty. "He and he only merits liberty who conquers it afresh from day to day."

Reprinted with permission from GREAT EXPRESSIONS OF HUMAN RIGHTS, *edited by R. M. MacIver and published by the Institute for Religious and Social Studies of the Jewish Theological Seminary of America in 1950.*

≺ III ≻

SOCIAL HISTORY

THE *importance of "the people" and the role of the individual in shaping the course of events is most readily apparent outside the large municipality. John Krout, reared in a small Midwestern town, well understands this. Because it became a principal theme of his historical writing, he found his professional eminence in the line of James Harvey Robinson and Dixon Ryan Fox as a social historian. His penetrating and suggestive review of the then new multi-volume* History of American Life *series, published by* The Macmillan Company, *1927–1944, to which he was himself an important contributor, is followed by examples of his work on the origins of prohibition, the turnpike era, and the history of American sport.*

Reflections of
a Social Historian

ABOUT thirty years ago James Harvey Robinson was patiently urging his fellow historians to forsake the error of their way. He was in revolt, however mild, against the conventional content and emphasis of historical writing in America. The antecedents of that revolt were numerous and complex, but a few of them seem obvious. Ernst Bernheim's *Lehrbuch* had stimulated his thinking about the nature and use of historical method. Impressed by the emphasis upon social and cultural factors in John Richard Green's *Short History of the English People*, he had turned to McMaster's volumes and found abundant evidence that the politico-military narratives had not exhausted the available material for the history of the United States. From his academic colleagues, particularly James T. Shotwell, and from experts in the natural sciences, he had received much inspiration, but he had not fallen completely under the spell of those who were certain that the laws of society could be written as precisely as the laws of physics. His quest was not immediately for the great generalization; he was anxious to help free the historians from the limitations and restrictions of their own history. Then, and then only, could

they seek ultimate explanations with some hope of finding them.

Robinson's state of mind is revealed in numerous essays,
especially those collected in 1912 in the slender volume
on *The New History*. He was insistent in reminding his
readers that history is not a field of knowledge sur-
rounded by barbed wire fences to keep out intruders,
but rather a genetic point of view which may be applied
with equal propriety to a piece of statuary or an economic depression, to the game of baseball or the House of
Commons. If the historian undertook to use this method
in examining "every trace and vestige of everything that
man has done or thought," he would need occasional assistance. Therefore, Robinson urged him to seek aid from
his natural allies—the geographers, the anthropologists,
the economists, the political scientists, and even the
sociologists. With such help he could make the interpretation, rather than the description, of historical data
his primary concern. In the fullness of time he might
even discover the trail travelled by human society and
chart its direction, without sacrificing accuracy and perspective to his own desire for what Alfred Whitehead
has called "a vision of the harmony of truth."

At the time that these views were elaborated they
seemed somewhat novel, but they probably owed much
to the scientific historians of the nineteenth century and
to the implications of the eighteenth century enlightenment. Some of their antecedents, as Professor Henry
Johnson has reminded us, are at least as old as the writings
of Herodotus. However that may be, the authors of
historical monographs and manuals in the United States

during the first decade of the present century were not guided by the principles which bulked so large in Robinson's thought. Formal instruction in history was largely confined to the political and economic narrative. The volumes of the *American Nation Series*, then in progress, were kept within proper constitutional and institutional limits, although Frederick J. Turner was permitted to discuss in the *Rise of the New West* phases of American life which apparently had significance only for the memorable years 1815–1830. At Johns Hopkins, Edward A. Freeman's much-quoted phrase, "History is past politics; and politics is present history," had faded on the wall of the seminary, but the "germ theory" of political institutions had lost little of its early vigor. At Yale, George Burton Adams was deeply distressed by the changing conceptions of the "field of history." When he spoke to the Christmas gathering of historians twenty-eight years ago, he warned his associates that they were about to lose their heritage. The well-defined preserve of history was being invaded by anthropologists, economists, and sociologists, who professed to be able to use historical data to answer such questions as: "What are the forces that determine human events and according to what laws do they act?" At Columbia, he who paused to listen could still hear reverberations, already growing faint, of John W. Burgess's dictum: It is only through law and institutions that social forces become in a large sense operative.

During the intervening years many a novelty has "flattened into a platitude." Much that was then heretical has become orthodox. The members of the American Historical Association, whatever their individual views concerning the perennial quest for law in history, can certainly agree that it is the historian's privilege to investigate anything which he finds interesting or important in mankind's past, and that it is not his responsibility to "guard the field of history" against possible raids by others busy with the analysis of social phenomena.

If the range of history has now become boundless, the individual expert has narrowed his activities. Within the guild there has been a rapid and continuing division of labor among the craftsmen, accelerated by personal preferences and by the demands of scholastic instruction. Too often the division seems to have been based upon the assumption that the colossal whole of history could be arranged in separable parts for convenient treatment by distinctive groups of specialists. Perhaps the so-called social historians have been most keenly aware of this assumption, for they generally have been regarded as the custodians of the "residuum" left after every other group has defined the boundaries of its interests. What the long-established craftsmen did not want for political history or diplomatic history or economic history, or some other "reputable" variety of history, remained as the stuff of social history.

For this situation the social historians themselves have been largely responsible. So much of their work reminded the reader—as Max Farrand once remarked—of the propensity of Lewis Carroll's Walrus

> To talk of many things;
> Of shoes—and ships—and sealing-wax—
> Of cabbages—and kings.

If the social historian seemed to be more concerned with particular curiosities than with social relationships, it was because of his desire to avoid gleaning in well-harvested fields. He did not insist that his discoveries were more important than the documents which reveal the genesis and development of institutions, or the statistics which indicate the trend of economic forces, but he sometimes advertised his "finds" with an enthusiasm which got the better of his judgment. Even his well-disposed friends found it difficult to suppress a smile when he announced with all the fervor of an antiquarian that he knew what the New Englander ate for breakfast in 1696, how brash young blades came to dance the polka, and when the horsehair sofa had won its conspicuous place in the conventional American parlor. The collection, however assiduous, of such interesting bits of information was not enough. The demand arose for a synthesis—not a formula sufficient to include the vast assortment of discrete facts collected, but a scheme for relating the materials so highly prized by the social historian to the conclusions of the historical specialists who had already found a center for their interests. In the *Rise of American Civilization* the Beards have given us a brilliant example of such a synthesis. With different emphasis and with more detailed illustrations the editors and authors of the *History of American Life* have presented a systematic description of the evolution of our present society.

As one reads the volumes in this cooperative series, it becomes clear that they do not represent an attempt to formulate or to illustrate a particular philosophy of history. No part of them is written, as considerable American history has been written, in "the shadow of St. Augustine." The authors are not engaged in a search for scientific laws of society which would satisfy a Buckle or a Lamprecht. They are not chiefly concerned with those metaphysical forces, which, in the words of Mr. Gladstone, "the tumult of our debates does not for a moment impede or disturb." Their primary objective is to describe the evolution of a particular society, to portray the social process here in America in terms generally ignored by students of political, economic, diplomatic, and military history. If there is little groping in these volumes for ultimate causation, there is much speculation concerning the proximate antecedents of events. Implicit throughout is the idea that the social process emerges from the thoughts, words, and deeds of men and women as they go about the routine of their daily lives. An imposing array of evidence is presented to show how Americans have proceeded from simple to complex forms in their work and in their recreation, in their personal concerns and in their public activities. If it be urged that such evidence, however convincingly arranged, is merely generalized description, the answer may well be that we need to know much about how the social process developed before we can do more than guess concerning its meaning and direction.

The choice of the chronological, rather than the topical, arrangement for the series has resulted in the division of the continuity of American history into segments in which a real or apparent unity exists. The early volumes conform to conventional division points in political history; the material for the later periods emphasizes the dominant ideas which have successively motivated American thought and action. Each author has endeavored, without minimizing or ignoring other contemporary ideas, to make a multiplicity of facts fit the particular theme which he has chosen for his period. An objective view of historical development, so far as that is humanly possible, has been maintained in selecting the various dominant themes. Certainly they do not reflect any editorial determination to arrange the facts in conformity with a particular interpretation of social evolution.

One may, however, raise certain specific questions concerning the dominant ideas which finally received editorial approval. The decades from 1830 to 1850 undoubtedly witnessed, among other things, the rise of the common man to a new stature in comparison with his fellows. But would it be difficult to portray the same years as an era of buoyant expansionism in which theories of our natural boundaries, our racial superiority, and our divinely appointed mission, so belligerently proclaimed in the halls of Congress, were exemplified by deeds along the Indian frontier, on the plains of Texas, in the valleys of the Sacramento and the Willamette? Was the rise of the common man but one manifestation of the temper of a generation profoundly stirred by the manifold implications of "Manifest Destiny"?

That much American history could be written in terms of a hesitant quest for social justice, few will deny. But there might be considerable disagreement if the attempt were made to select the years in which that quest became a dominant motivation. Did it constitute the unifying principle in the period between 1898 and 1914? Or was the continuing theme of those years the growing power of corporate wealth in every phase of the nation's life? Of that power Professor Faulkner is well aware. The data appear in his volume. By a slightly different arrangement and emphasis he could have presented another picture of the first decade of the twentieth century which would have been equally significant as social history and equally representative of his "objective" approach to the evidence. The problem is not peculiar to this series, or to the content of social history. It is an insistent problem in all historical writing, lately advanced by some among us as a pretext for abandoning the attempt to attain an objective point of view.

Historians have ever been inclined to read the past in the light of their own experience, a natural inclination which cannot easily be escaped. Yet it tends to distort our view of historical processes. In the volumes here under consideration there has been little yielding to that present-mindedness which seeks to reduce complexity to simplicity and confusion to order. None of the authors has approached his particular segment of time with a determination to find ideas and events which are peculiarly significant for the present. Society in seventeenth century America is not described against the background of twentieth century standards and interests. In the post-Civil War decades those intellectual currents are emphasized which had meaning at that time, regardless of their validity today. There are a few instances, but only a few, of measuring the importance of past events with a gauge better suited for the present than for the past.

Each author has attempted to describe that which seemed precious in the social life of the era of which he writes. Such descriptions have much more meaning for him who would understand our evolution than patterns based upon those manifestations of the past behavior of Americans which neatly fit in with our immediate, contemporary interests.

There is gratifying evidence that the editors and authors are aware of their particular province as a part of the life of the western world. This is true not only of the volumes which deal with the centuries when Europeans were transplanting their civilization into a strange wilderness, but also of the later accounts concerned with the fruits of that transplanting. One finds numerous examples of the interchange of ideas and skills between Europe and America during the provincial years, an interchange which profoundly affected the life of a people, whom Franklin described as just beginning to "afford leisure to cultivate the finer arts and improve the common stock of knowledge." Poor Richard's American Philosophical Society owed much to the inspiration of learned societies across the Atlantic. The international aspects of the "Great Awakening" stand forth, revealing contemporary religious movements in Great Britain, in the German provinces, and throughout the English colonies, movements in which the preaching of Edwards and Whitefield attained more than provincial significance. This mutuality of experience is further exemplified in Carl Russell Fish's discussions of the humanitarian reforms, which flourished on both sides of the Atlantic at mid-nineteenth century, and of the "wave of intellectual romanticism" whose variants were but slightly affected by international boundaries. That the "vogue of realism," which intrigues the historian of modern Europe, influenced the thought of Americans is abundantly evident in the volumes by Nevins, Schlesinger, and Slosson. It has often been remarked that the social history of the United States cannot be written until the social history of Europe has been written. It may be added that many writers of American social history have not always utilized efficiently the available knowledge of European history. Such knowledge, in the first place, is valuable as the "background" for phases of American life which are commonly regarded as aspects of an indigenous culture. Of course, that background should not be confined to a prelude to the exploration and colonization of the sixteenth and seventeenth centuries. The fact that we know more about the England which produced John Winthrop than about the Prussian province whence the youthful Carl Schurz fled is symptomatic of one of our difficulties in appraising the social results of European immigration in the nineteenth century. It is a difficulty which remains unresolved in this series. The foreigners' contribution to our material well-being and to our intellectual and cultural interests is not slighted, but the need still exists for a deeper probing into the life of the communities whence these folk came and the nature of the "mental furniture" which they brought with them.

Furthermore, an understanding of the European scene is important for purposes of comparison. There is a hint of this sort of comparative study—but it is only a hint—in Fish's volume. While Americans were occupying the great central plain of the Mississippi Valley, and bringing the Pacific slope within the orbit of their influence, Englishmen were undertaking a similar adventure in Australia and New Zealand, and Russians were moving slowly eastward across the Siberian steppe. At the time there was little, if any, "mutual exchange of experimentation," but it is well worth the social historian's while to compare the different methods and the variations in results. In political history the comparative method has been enlightening; why should it not be equally so in studying such nonpolitical groups as business corporations, trade unions, temperance societies, private schools, women's clubs, and research foundations.

Although the frontier is not discussed in this series as a world phenomenon, its influence on American society is fully recognized. The record, unfortunately, is fragmentary, for the volumes dealing with the years from 1763 to 1830 are still to be published. But the main tenets of the Turner thesis appear—the frontier as a social force, promoting democracy here and in Europe, providing a potential safety-valve for every form of discontent, operating in the direction of rapid and effective Americanization, and creating an opportunity for recurrent social experimentation. In these volumes there is a wealth of material illustrating the transit of our civilization, which supplements the work of Turner. The argument, it seems to me, is notably advanced. Wertenbaker and Adams are concerned with three periods of cultural evolution: first, the slow modification of European standards among a people struggling for existence in the wilderness; second, a period of rather rapid decline, marked by confused attempts to maintain earlier standards; and third, the growth of a native culture, characterized by indigenous as well as transplanted features. How much was indigenous, and how much merely transplanted, remains in doubt.

Perhaps one would invite considerable controversy by insisting that this formula, which seems valid for the seventeenth and eighteenth centuries, is equally applicable to the communities occupied by Americans in the nineteenth. Yet something similar to these three stages may be observed on successive frontiers in the Mississippi Valley and the Far West. Civilization, we are reminded, tends to decline "when it strikes the frontier." In many respects the cultural level of Massachusetts in the time of Cotton Mather's youth was not so high as it had been in the days of John Cotton. It rose again, however, in the generation of Thomas Hutchinson. He who has the patience to winnow the wheat of local histories soon finds evidence of this decline and revival. Seneca County in Ohio, for example, apparently had more college graduates in its population in 1825 than in 1850. Within a decade the number had risen, as native sons returned from Eastern schools to join the alumni of the newly established college —Heidelberg—at the county seat. From legal records, the value of which for social history has been stressed by Professor Randall, one learns that the requirements for admission to the legal profession were higher in 1830 than they were thirty years later. Perhaps much of the general lowering of standards, which seems to mark the three decades before the Civil War, was but the influence of communities where the second generation was failing to maintain the tone set by the original settlers.

From frontier areas as well as from older communities the individual and group carriers of artistic and professional competence forwarded the "transit of civilization" in America. Here is the point at which the *History of American Life* has made its most distinctive contribution to the understanding of our social history. Its pages contain innumerable examples of the advance and retreat of cultural influences, the slow and uncertain differentiation of functions, and the emergence of specialized services and skills. The medical practitioner at the close of the seventeenth century was poorly trained by comparison with the physicians who had migrated from England fifty years earlier, yet some progress had been made in functional differentiation. Healing the body was less frequently associated with the duties of the clergyman, in what Cotton Mather once described as an "angelic conjunction." Within a few decades some communities were offering financial support sufficient to attract competent physicians from Europe. Virginia welcomed John Mitchell of the Royal Society in 1700; Dr. William Douglass, educated at Leyden and Paris, found opportunities in Boston in 1718; Cadwallader Colden, trained at Edinburgh, gained distinction in New York. In time the physician, who had already forgotten his career as a barber, could abandon his functions as a dispenser of drugs and an extractor of teeth. Then came the slow development of specialization within the profession, the emergence of the surgeon, the diagnostician, the pathologist, the dermatologist, and a host of others. This differentiation goes forward in many lines. The colonial printer was a "multiple functionary." One need not turn to the many-sided Franklin, who was unique. Even the ordinary printer set type, prepared copy, wrote editorial opinions, bought and sold books, and occasionally managed a small circulating library. He was progenitor of the editor, the reporter, the publisher, the book dealer, and the advertising agency. Likewise, from the interests of the general naturalist, represented in the eighteenth century by James Logan, Cadwallader Colden, and John Bartram, have come such specialties as the botany of Asa Gray, the ichthyology of Louis Agassiz, the geology of James Dwight Dana, the physical chemistry of Willard Gibbs, and the embryology of Edmund Wilson, to mention only a few.

The fascinating record of this evolution from simplicity to complexity, from composite functions to specialized skills, is here set forth with amazing detail. It will be even more richly illustrated, when the two volumes, now lacking, are published. Such a record provides an arrangement for bringing many discrete facts into a convenient relation. It does not, as Dixon Ryan Fox has well emphasized, explain the social process. The reader may still raise many questions only partially discussed in this series. Why, for instance, did the process of differentiation move more rapidly at one time than at another? Is the rate of acceleration constantly increasing? How close is the correlation between a highly organized economic system and a high cultural level? By what means has the skill of the specialist been carried from Europe to America, and from one part of this country to another? By accidental individual carriers? By selective imitation? By group missionary zeal? Have sectional antagonisms retarded specialization in certain areas? How much has the rivalry of classes for power and prestige speeded up the tempo of social change? These and many similar questions receive here some attention, but they need to be much more carefully investigated. Surprisingly inadequate is the discussion of the geographic bases of sectionalism and the social consequences of a continuing adaptation to the physical environment.

In the pageant of the fine arts, which in these volumes too often becomes a mere catalogue of names and events, the man of property has played a conspicuous part. His influence during the eighteenth century has been properly emphasized by Adams. We see the support accorded to painters, musicians, actors, and architect-builders as wealth concentrated in the hands of the merchants of the seaport towns and the planters and land speculators of the southern tidewater. The Waldos, Livingstons, Morrises, Byrds, and Ravenels, and scores of other families, made possible the work of Robert Feke, Alexander Gordon, Lewis Hallam, and John Singleton Copley. If the eighteenth century was marked by the degradation of folk art, it also witnessed the growth of artistic accumulations by the upper classes.

Somewhat more than a century later the economic structure had become immensely complex, yet Nevins and Schlesinger and Faulkner managed to give us a picture, occasionally blurred and indistinct, of the industrial capitalist moving with much energy, if little discrimination, to determine canons of taste and artistic appreciation. One searches in vain, however, for a comparable portrait of the merchant-capitalist who flourished in the years between the decline of the "tie-wig" aristocracy and the rise of the industrial plutocracy. For the decade of the fifties Cole has sketched an outline of the interests of the commercial class, but the significant rôle of the merchant-capitalist is not clearly revealed. Whether he was accumulating riches in an eastern seaport or adventuring in new communities in the Mississippi Valley, his activities bulked large in determining the cultural interests of the group. In many a Western settlement his general store, grist mill, saw mill, and distillery became the nucleus for a rapidly growing village which soon was able to support the competence of the teacher, clergyman, lawyer, and doctor, even if it could make little pretense to an appreciation of the fine arts. Into the hands of the merchant came the produce of the countryside. He conducted a produce exchange, extended credit widely, and engaged in an irregular banking business which enabled him to guide the economy of the neighboring farmlands. As his dollars went into town lots, canal stock, and railroad securities, so his ideas went into the conventional codes of manners and morals and set the standards determining that which was beautiful and true. A Josiah Hedges in the village of Tiffin near Lake Erie was as much interested in civic affairs as an Arthur Tappan in New York City—and gave of his profits to support humanitarian enterprises as generously as did the New Yorker. Many a group of reformers in the "yeasty thirties" and "roaring forties" would have been less articulate without the financial aid of merchant-capitalists—West and East.

The plain folk of the soil have been even less adequately portrayed than the representatives of the mercantile class at mid-nineteenth century. There is no description of the typical small farm in the Northern states, comparable to Cole's delineation of the *antebellum* cotton plantation, or Nevins's vivid sketch of the ranch of the cattle country, or Schlesinger's photographic scenes of Xenia, Ohio. Yet an understanding of the routine and spirit of the old farm, in the days before the clanking of machines had become loud on its acres, is of primary importance in any appraisal of American life during the generation before the Civil War. The available material is embarrassingly abundant; bulky files of the agricultural journals constitute a revelation of the mind of rural America. Although these files are cited several times, there is little evidence that their riches have been effectively mined.

But one hesitates to protest that any detail is lacking in a series so elaborately furnished with descriptive data. The encyclopedic range of the authors' interests is matched by their determination to let no bibliographic aid escape. In the main the monographic literature, much of it written during the last quarter century, and the primary sources have been used with discriminating care. One is compelled to make an exception in the case of the volume dealing with the *Nationalizing of Business*. In a few instances, the author bases her discussion upon accounts now superseded; more frequently she fails to analyze carefully the monographic literature which she uses. There is little evidence that she is aware of the concentration of financial power and its social implications. The omissions are doubly disappointing, since the period from 1878 to 1898 is a crucial one, and this particular volume was designed to supplement the phases presented in the *Rise of the City*.

Unlike many coöperative works the present one achieves a coherence which does not rest exclusively upon cross references ingeniously inserted in the footnotes. Against the foil of McMaster's attempt to fuse social with political and economic factors, its virtues stand brightly forth. For the social historian it performs the service of challenging certain current impressions, though it might well have gone farther. It helps to correct the notion that the social historian deals only with the embroidery around the edge of substantial material; that he minimizes or ignores the data of political, diplomatic, and even economic history in reaching his conclusions; that he naïvely makes moral judgments as if he were recording the result of scientific observations; and that he has a predilection for simple explanations of complex phenomena. One puts these ten volumes aside with a feeling of having witnessed the development of a "great booming confusion," the various aspects of which have been carefully described. Perhaps that is the meaning of our history during the three hundred and thirty years since Jamestown. Or, will further studies of this general type, if there is more daring in the search for a dynamic principle, finally reveal to us the direction in which we have been travelling?

Reprinted with permission from W. E. Lingelbach, ed., APPROACHES TO AMERICAN SOCIAL HISTORY (*New York, Appleton-Century, 1937*).

Glimpses of a
Golden Age

F R O M the day in 1642 that William Bradford confided to his journal his astonishment at the growth of drunkenness among the Puritans, efforts to put down drinking by law have been unceasing in America. John Winthrop tried to persuade himself by means of a faultless syllogism that statutes against the vice were workable and wholesome, but his fellow Puritans, even in that pious day, were not ready to abandon it. Rather, they seemed bent on indulging themselves freely, and thereby they achieved for themselves a whispered reputation for ardent and even excessive devotion to the bowl. That habit has been ascribed by their descendants to various circumstances: to the hereditary influence of a hard-drinking Anglo-Saxon ancestry, to the hardship and exposure of frontier life, to the universal contemporary belief in the medicinal properties of alcohol, and, finally, to the cruelly ascetic character of Puritanism, which forced the individual to seek relief from his religious exercises in the joys of the cup. Each explanation affords an opportunity for interesting speculation; all are significant because they rest alike upon the hypothesis that heavy drinking was the rule rather than the exception among the Puritans.

Whether the hypothesis be true or not, the Fathers seem to have convicted their own generation. By their writings their fellows stand indicted. Intemperance, resulting from the flagrant abuse of "nature's gift," conflicted with the Calvinistic idea that alcohol was given to man for the benefit of the community and not for the voluptuous gratification of individual appetites. Therefore, by moral precept and statutory provision, the ban was placed upon drunkenness. He who stepped over the shadowy line of moderation was an outcast. His pathway was in side streets and back alleys; summary punishment was his lot if he dared to parade his joy on the main highways. Even the way of the merely prospective transgressor was hard. If he repaired to the public-house for his liquor, he was watched carefully. Unless his previous conduct had been good, he might learn to his sorrow that his name was on the list of those denied the right to purchase any liquor at all. If he got intoxicants and drank unwisely, he was likely to fall into the clutches of the constables. His first offense brought a fine, usually five shillings, or, in default of payment, a sojourn of from one to six hours in the stocks. In case his tippling became habitual, he could be whipped or forced to wear some mark of his shame. At the discretion of the magistrates his kind were frequently put to work on the fortifications, or assigned to some other task that would save money for the town.

In the Middle Atlantic and Southern colonies the lawmakers frowned almost as fiercely upon intemperance

as did those of New England. That it might be less difficult for the justices to detect offenders, Maryland in
1639 defined drunkenness as "drinking with excess to the
notable perturbation of any organ of sense or motion."
From everyone discovered in such a state the Lord Proprietor was to receive a fine of five shillings. If the guilty
party chanced to be a servant, corporal punishment or
confinement in the stocks for twenty-four hours was the
penalty. The experience of a few years demonstrated that
servants were not the only incorrigibles, and in 1658
the suffrage was taken from all freeholders who were
convicted for the third time. None of the neighboring
colonies was quite so severe in the penalties inflicted, but
all provided a fine or the stocks for first offenders, and
hard labor or whippings for recidivists.

It is doubtful whether such laws were as strictly en-
forced in the plantation provinces as among the Puritans.
In the social intercourse of the South there was not that
compelling concern about the conduct of the other fellow that so generally permeated New England thought
and action. The authorities were apt to be lenient. Moreover, had they been ever so vigilant, they could not have
matched the efficiency with which their colleagues of
New England detected offenders. Take North Carolina
as an example. According to the law of that colony, a
person could be convicted of drunkenness only if seen
in his cups by a justice of the peace, or on the oath of
one or more eyewitnesses, and the information was
worthless unless presented within ten days of the offense.
In view of the sparsely settled character of the colony
and the difficulties of communication, it is probable that

many escaped even the most conscientious servants of the law. In the more populous colony of Virginia conditions seem to have been different. Proof that serious efforts to suppress drunkenness there were made during the seventeenth century has been exhumed by P. A. Bruce, the most distinguished student of the early social life of the colony. His numerous citations from the records of the county courts closely resemble the entries in the early records of the Massachusetts General Court, when almost every session witnessed several presentments for intemperance. Although these entries do not reveal an ideal state of enforcement, they are sufficient to indicate that the law against drunkenness was certainly not a dead letter.

In the aggregate these prosecutions seem to cast a considerable doubt upon the sobriety of the American colonists. There are witnesses, however, to answer the accusation. Governor Berkeley did not hesitate to inform the Commissioners for Foreign Plantations that he considered the Virginia planters generally more temperate than English gentlemen. John Winthrop recorded with evident satisfaction that at a great training at Boston in 1641, when 1200 men drilled for two days, not one case of drunkenness was observed, although the supply of wine, small beer, and other liquors was abundant. An observer of Massachusetts life during the middle years of the same century found little evidence of intemperance, even in the busier towns of the seaboard. And as late as 1686 Judge Samuel Sewall, who was extremely sensitive to every public disturbance, could write of a few townsmen who had become boisterous over their drinks that such highhanded wickedness had hardly been heard of before in Boston. Doubtless there were similar parties of which the worthy judge was not cognizant, but they were not numerous enough to make Boston a disorderly town. Indeed, against the dark background of England at the opening of the eighteenth century, town life in America stood out as a model of orderliness and sobriety. It was the time when the residents of London feared to venture abroad after dark unless protected by armed retainers. Gangs of drunken ruffians roamed the dark streets at night, setting upon all they met, not even excepting the officers of the watch. Young men of the nobility, as well as servants and apprentices, committed wanton outrages upon sober citizens with entire impunity. Drunkenness was rampant in its most disgusting forms. The colonies were sober and decorous by comparison. No bands of the vicious made the streets of Charleston or Williamsburg or New Haven terrors for the late straggler. The immediate descendants of Judge Sewall would have been as surprised as he at any unseemly disturbance in Boston.

But the eighteenth century was not many years old when a change came over the scene. It was caused largely by the increasing popularity of distilled spirits in general, and rum in particular. The earliest settlers had brought to the New World a decided preference for wines and malt liquors, a preference which they sought to gratify by domestic production of their favorite drinks, thus supplementing the importations from Europe. Skill was required in the making of palatable ale or beer, and good

brewers and maltsters were greatly in demand in all the
settlements. Malt houses were early established in New
England, but in spite of the fact that the towns encouraged them, successful maltsters were rare. The con-
sequent scarcity of high quality malt was a constant
handicap to the brewing industry. Virginia, Maryland,
and New England supplemented the domestic production by importations of barley and beer from the Dutch
settlements on the Hudson and the Delaware, but the
supply of malt liquors was not adequate to meet the
ever-growing demand.

Many of the colonists were confident that in time the
New World would surpass the Old in the production of
wines. French vine growers were sent to Virginia in
1621 by the London Company to instruct the people in
the cultivation of grapes, but their efforts seem to have
been futile, for forty years later Thomas Woodward,
surveyor of Albemarle county in Carolina, estimated that
if the Virginians had been able to produce their own
wines they would have possessed a greater per capita
wealth than that of the most opulent country in Europe.
Woodward, accordingly, encouraged the Carolina proprietors in their purpose to make the colony a wine-
producing country. Wild grapes grew in such abundance
in Georgia that the trustees endeavored to establish viti-
culture. Cuttings of malmsey from Maderia and tubs of
vines from Burgundy were sent to ambitious landholders
in the colony. Although a few succeeded in cultivating
the vines and making a sweet wine, most found the experiment unprofitable. But faith in the ultimate success
of such projects persisted, for in 1700 the Earl of Bello-

mont assured the Lords of Trade that it was possible to produce enough wine in the continental colonies to supply all the dominions of the Crown. He cited as evidence the wild grapes which grew in great profusion along the Hudson River and were palatable in spite of their wildness. The successful French vineyards in the neighborhood of Montreal convinced him that New York was not too far north. Besides, he had tasted wine produced in the Narragansett country in Rhode Island, where the climate was not unlike that of the upper Hudson valley. But Bellomont's enthusiasm was not borne out by any actual results. Although groups of Palatine refugees, expert vine dressers, were settled in Virginia, the Carolinas, and along the Hudson during the eighteenth century, the natural handicaps of climate and soil were too much for their skill, and native wines seldom replaced the imported on the colonial gentleman's table.

One drink of domestic production that achieved a well-merited popularity was apple cider. Foreign travelers found that it ranked with the best drinks to which they were accustomed. Wherever they journeyed, from Boston to Savannah, it was served by the individual host and at the public inns. In 1663 Josselyn enjoyed it, spiced and sweetened, at the taphouses in Boston. Hugh Jones declared that the Virginia cider was not much inferior to that of Herefordshire, if kept until the proper age, but no one seemed able to keep it. The Labadist missionaries, Dankaerts and Sluyter, considered the New York cider the best they had encountered during their travels in 1679 and 1680. During the seventeenth century the New England colonies produced great quantities of the beverage. Henry Wolcott, of Windsor, Connecticut, had an extensive orchard from which he got annually nearly five hundred hogsheads. In 1648, when he began to sell, the price was 2s. 8d. a gallon, but thirty years later production had so increased that he was forced to sell at 10s. a barrel. The constant addition of new orchards sent the price down still further, until in 1700 anything above 6s. was a fair return.

Although the use of hard cider thus became universal, imported wines were much in demand among those who could afford them. Madeira was the favorite, while next in popular esteem came claret, port, canary, and burgundy. Brandy, malaga, and sherry also enjoyed a limited vogue. In fact, almost every wine of merit was to be found on the tables of the wealthier classes and in the bars of the more pretentious taverns. Though individual tastes differed, people of fortune in New England were generally partial to canary in preference to the harsher madeira, which was the favorite in the Middle Atlantic and Southern colonies. It was canary upon which Judge Sewall relied to win the favor of his lady love, and he was pleased when it was served at the weddings he attended. But Josiah Quincy, when he visited Virginia and the Carolinas in 1773, found there the richest wines he had ever tasted and thought them better than the varieties commonly served in Massachusetts. Peter Kalm, the Swedish naturalist, and Adam Gordon, the Scotch peer, were equally generous in their praise of the vintages drunk by the merchants and planters south of the Hudson. Kalm was particularly interested in the native wines, which were still in the experimental stage. In Pennsylvania and Maryland he drank excellent beverages made from blackberries, cherries, and wild grapes, but he considered peach brandy, used extensively in all the colonies, "not good for people who have a more refined taste, but only for the common kind of people, such as workmen and the like." Burnaby thought that the imitation burgundy of Maryland, which he drank at the table of Governor Hamilton of Pennsylvania, was not bad "for the first trial."

In 1759 Israel Acrelius, provost of the Swedish churches in America, made a survey of the congregations under his control, and had an excellent opportunity to observe the everyday habits of the communities he visited. In his record more than thirty drinks, all well known at the time, are listed and described. Beside the wines already noticed, various mixed drinks are mentioned: punch, flip, sling, mead, and sillibub. The latter, made by adding milk and sugar to wine, was long a favorite as a cooling beverage in the Summer. Punch usually consisted of lemon or lime juice and Jamaica spirits, diluted with sweetened water. It was the popular drink for all social gatherings at which the thirst of a large number had to be satisfied. Flip and sling were variations of a single ingredient, Jamacia or New England rum. The former, containing small beer, rum, and brown sugar, was served after a hot poker had been thrust in to give it a bitter flavor, while the latter was a simple concoction, half rum and half water, sweetened to the taste. Mead, of ancient fame in England, was prepared by allowing honey and water to ferment. The colonists also had a strong beer of American brew, porter, and bottled beer from England, and a fermentation of honey and yeast, known as metheglin.

More significant than any enumeration of drinks is the revelation, contained in Acrelius' list, that rum had become the chief stimulant of the Americans by 1759. When the New England trade with Barbados commenced, shortly after 1650, the product of the colonists' small stills was supplanted by a more satisfying distillation from the West Indies. Molasses, brought by adventurous traders from England's island possessions to the merchants of Connecticut and Massachusetts, later supplied the ingredient necessary for a large-scale domestic production of rum. Although the New England liquor never equalled that of the West Indies, it was produced more cheaply and soon became popular in all the colonies. Men engaged in the hard labor of forest and field, and fisher folk, constantly following the sea, demanded a strong stimulant to lighten the burden of their toil. As the demand for rum increased, more merchants ventured to risk their surplus in the business of distilling, until almost every town possessed a still house of its own. Some manufactured solely for local consumption, but larger establishments were not lacking in the important trade centers of Rhode Island, Connecticut, and Massachusetts. Newport, during the eighteenth century, grew rich from its distilleries, and the product of the Medford firms was far-famed. While the industry was largely concentrated in the New England colonies, New York, Pennsylvania, and the Carolinas also boasted establishments. Philadelphia rum was pronounced as good as that of New England, and commanded an equal price in the market. New York City combined distillation with sugar refining. Indeed, the multiplication of distilleries was chiefly responsible for the change which came over colonial industry during the first half of the eighteenth century, a change marked by notable social and economic consequences.

Whether the liquor then drunk was of domestic or foreign origin, it penetrated deeply into the social life of the Americans. Rum seemed to be ubiquitous. It was found in the finest tavern and the vilest pot house. The traveler seldom journeyed far enough to escape it, even in the mountains of the frontier. People of fortune kept a stock of good quality in their homes, while the servant and common laborer regarded it as indispensable. Parents gave it to their children for many of the minor ills of childhood, and it was regarded as a useful medicine for almost all diseases. Nothing else was capable of satisfying so many human needs. It contributed to the success of any festive occasion and inspirited those in sorrow and distress. It gave courage to the soldier, endurance to the traveler, foresight to the statesman, and inspiration to the preacher. It sustained the sailor and the plowman, the trader and the trapper. By it were lighted the fires of revelry and devotion. Few doubted that it was a great boon to mankind.

Church, as well as home festivities, were made the merrier by liberal potations of the "good creature." The building of a new edifice, the installation of new pews, and especially the ordination of a new minister were occasions when slight restriction was placed upon the appetite. In Boston John Vyall was requested to keep a house near the Second Church, that thirsty sinners, going to hear John Mayo or Increase Mather preach, might be satisfied. The ordination ceremony for the Rev. Phineas Stevens at Contocook, New Hampshire, October 29, 1740, required nineteen gallons of rum, but only six drinking glasses. The vestries of certain Episcopal churches met at the tavern, where the chief business transacted was the consumption of good rum at the expense of the congregation. To the tavern also resorted the town selectmen and the country justices, that the business of government might have the benefit of the clarifying influence of ardent spirits. There, over a bowl of toddy or a mug of flip, matters of concern were decided, and civil and criminal cases were heard.

The tavern, of course, was the most important factor in the colonial liquor traffic. Though there was a vast difference in architectural form between the stately King's Arms in Boston and the rude wooden shack which served as a public house in the back country of North Carolina, both were symbols of an influence widely felt in eighteenth century America. They represented not only the performance of a public service for private profit, but also the strengthening of bonds of unity within and between communities. As centrally located as either the town hall or the meeting house, the tavern in New England served as a sort of community center, housing in cases of emergency the worshipping congregation or the voters assembled for town meeting. To it came the traveler from distant parts, bringing his welcome news of unusual occurrences and interesting experiences of the journey, and receiving in return an account of local happenings with which to regale his audience at the next stop. Town idlers loved to gather on Saturday afternoons in the great room near the bar and listen to the discussions of politics, religion, and current events. Often the conversation was of more than passing interest, for politicians used these informal gatherings to discuss issues and select candidates. Such was the nature of the meetings at the Raleigh in Williamsburg, which have forever associated that tavern with the cause of American independence.

Training days, county court sessions, town meetings, and convocations were seasons of extraordinary business and profit for the owner of the public house. Those who attended a muster, with appetites whetted by the liquor doled out at the officers' expense, were generous in their patronage at the bar after the day's drilling was finished. Officers and men mingled in good comradeship, and toasts were drunk to everyone in authority from the governor to the company captain. Newly appointed officers were expected to wet their commissions by liberal purchases of liquor for the men. Boisterousness, rowdyism, and rough and tumble fighting were characteristic of the sessions of the county court, and occasionally the temptation of the tavern's good cheer was too much for even the presiding justices. The colonist journeyed to the county seat on such occasions with no idea of devoting his time entirely to matters of law and business. Usually he had traveled a considerable distance over roads that made the trip anything but pleasant, and he was bent upon making merry for several days as compensation for the hardships of the journey. In the South horse racing, cockfighting, and wrestling matches, mingled with much gambling and hard drinking, were favorite diversions after the demands of justice had been satisfied.

It was from the tavern, as a rule, that the colonial householder got his supply of liquor. A few fortunate individuals, such as Colonel William Byrd of Virginia, could indulge their love of conspicuous consumption by importing the best wines and brandies directly from Europe, but for the majority this was an impossibility. Often traders, calling themselves wholesalers, purchased hogsheads of rum and spirits from the merchant-importers in the larger towns and traveled up and down the countryside, selling their stock in five and ten gallon lots. Such a dealer was Joshua Hempstead during the first quarter of the eighteenth century. He has left in his diary a detailed statement of the manner in which he supplied his Connecticut neighbors with their year's supply of rum. Most families, however, influenced either by loyalty to the local taverner or by the necessity of buying in small quantities, made their purchases at the public house.

John Dunton tells us that jovial George Monck made the Blue Anchor at Boston a delight to the most fastidious. His place was famed far and wide for the beauty of its special rooms and the excellence of its fare. Alexander Hamilton, the Maryland physician, closely observing manners and customs as he visited the northern colonies in 1744, found much to praise in the New York taverns, though the people frequenting them were extremely annoying. More often, however, the record left by the critical traveler is a severe denunciation of both taverns and tavern keepers. Birket considered the New England houses either "very indifferent" or "intolerably dirty," and his experiences with the proprietors caused him to seek refuge in a private home wherever possible. His unfavorable opinion is paralleled by that of William Logan in regard to the region south of Pennsylvania. Called to South Carolina by business, Logan rode down the coast from New Jersey to Charleston, noting in his journal as he progressed the sort of entertainment he encountered from day to day. With the exception of a few good houses in Virginia, the farther south he journeyed the worse he fared. "Poor liquor," "dirty food," and "nasty rooms" are frequent entries in his account of the trip.

Although the accommodations were thus often unsatisfactory, the number of taverns everywhere was large. A group of Moravian brethren, making their way through the back country from Bethlehem, Pennsylvania, to Wachovia, North Carolina, experienced little difficulty, in 1753, in finding an inn of some sort during the course of every day's journey. In the sparsely settled sections, to be sure, these inns were usually nothing more than licensed private houses. One petitioner in Western Virginia urged his case on the ground that he was "very much infested with travelers" and needed a license to save himself from their impositions. Establishments of such a character seldom pretended to satisfy the needs of the guest in a professional fashion. He simply shared what the family ordinarily enjoyed in the way of food and lodging. His host probably provided cider, if he was ambitious enough to cultivate an orchard, and a cheap grade of rum.

In the eastern communities, particularly in New England, the host of the public house enjoyed considerable prestige. The towns from the beginning presented men of good reputation to be licensed by the justices, and the tradition continued well into the eighteenth century. Cambridge was long served by the most prominent deacon in the church, and upon his retirement his son succeeded him. The tendency to license the same person year after year vested the calling with dignity. The high esteem in which it was held is evident from the pages of the early Harvard records, on which the names of students were listed not alphabetically, but according to the relative social position of their families. In the class of 1653 Joshua Long, son of an English innkeeper, precedes Samuel Whiting, whose father was a clergyman. John Harriman, son of a prominent taverner at New Haven, led the son of the Rev. Peter Hobart on the roster of the class of 1667. It was not unusual, indeed, for the town clerk, the deputy to the General Court, or the justice of the peace in Massachusetts to round off a public career by getting a license to run a public house.

But during the eighteenth century the ancient craft lost caste rapidly. Sons of tavern keepers failed to retain their high rank on the college rolls at Harvard. The courts began to award licenses with a greater liberality, which meant a rapid decline in the type of men licensed. Many widows were granted permission to keep public houses, that they might not become dependent upon the community. In some localities persons of influence obtained licenses and then employed agents to conduct the business, that they might escape responsibility for any scandal connected with it. This practice became common in the middle and southern colonies, where the aristocratic host, considerate of his good name, was replaced by a horde of unscrupulous keepers of rude huts. No reproach, however, attached to the proprietor of a reputable house. At the close of the Revolution a considerable number of officers sought to recoup their fortunes, financially and politically, by entering a business that was profitable and kept them constantly before the public. In the closing decade of the century an English visitor was impressed by the number of lawyers, ex-judges, and former members of the legislature who kept taverns in New York State. His observations convinced him that the lawyer and the taverner had found the open sesame to riches and honor in the newer communities of the country. Nevertheless, neither the reflected glory of a military reputation nor the prestige of a judicial career could restore the occupation to its former high place. Gradually it went down hill. By the opening of the nineteenth century the old-time tavern had already become the saloon.

Reprinted with permission from THE AMERICAN MER-CURY, *5:208–14, June, 1925.*

The Turnpike Era

T H E young republic in 1790 desperately needed roads. Boundless possibilities were locked within the wilderness that still overlapped most of the original states and stretched toward the Mississippi; but natural resources would become goods only when men could get at them, use them, take them to other men. Distances, which in human terms meant time and effort, were the curse of the country and would continue so to be until dissolved in large part by engineering science. Till this could be accomplished the very integrity of the nation was in danger. The conquest of distance, quite as much as technical advance in production, was to revolutionize American life.

No striking improvement had occurred in travel, and therefore communication, since man learned the art of spreading cloth to catch the power of the wind. Nature's pathways, the ocean and the far-reaching streams and lakes, were used wherever possible. To go by water was far cheaper and more convenient than to go by land. But there were uncertainties that would irritate the modern traveler. The applicant must first find some skipper whose plans happened to match his own. Even then, the arrival date could be but roughly guessed. A traveler facing December winds spent eighteen days sailing from Eastport, Maine, to Portsmouth, New Hampshire, whereas the following June he did it in two days. The hundred and fifty miles of navigation on the Hudson took three days when the weather favored, but a week was often needed and sometimes a fortnight. By 1820 large craft covering long distances made faster time, going from Boston to Charleston in good weather in less than two weeks and at a cost of fifteen dollars.

Land traffic picked its tedious course as best it could. There was not a soundly paved road in the country when the federal government was set up. Moreover, travel still wound its way, in large part, in shadow. The steady chopping of a hundred years had pushed the frontier line well up the Atlantic slope, but even near the sea immense unbroken areas remained. Count Volney declared that in his journeys of 1796, including that from Boston to Richmond, he traveled scarce three miles together on cleared land. "Everywhere I found the roads, or rather paths, bordered and overshadowed with coppices or tall trees . . . ," and he spoke feelingly of "the tormenting swarm of breeze-flies, moschettoes and gnats." Young Francis Baily, fresh from London, found it similarly gloomy: "To travel day after day, among trees a hundred feet high, is oppressive to a degree which those cannot conceive who have not experienced it." But, despite this general picture, much of the way ran through cultivated farm land, marked by zigzag rail fences, a quick expedient where wood and land were cheap. In New England and New York the road was often flanked by dry stone walls, the slow laborious combing of the glaciated fields having thus turned a nuisance into a utility.

Along the highway passed the procession of life in its infinite variety. Many trudged afoot, with burdens or without. Many went on horseback. On Sabbath mornings there might be placed behind the saddle a leather-covered cushion, or pillion, for the wife in best bonnet and kerchief bound for church. On remote wood paths pack trains of from two to twenty horses, generally of stunted breed, trucked their wares through the sparsely settled country, each pair of balanced panniers holding nearly two hundred pounds. Furs and hides were the usual staples on the townward journey; hardware and various small goods had their place as the train threaded its way back into the forest. Hawkers were ubiquitous. There were drug and notion peddlers like the one Hawthorne pictured a little later in his *American Note-Books*. Glib, insinuating, and of easy honesty, he found wide markets for New England's manufactures, but too often left behind him a prejudice against the Yankee as a "slick one." Even Timothy Dwight, stout champion of New England virtues, deplored the tin peddler: "Many of the young men, employed in this business, part, at an early period with both modesty, and principle."

In contrast to the peddlers were the loud-mouthed wagoners, each guiding the four- or six-horse team that hauled his great blue and red wagon. Boatlike in shape, with front and back wheels close together and its deep box rising fore and aft to keep the load from sliding whether the journey lay uphill or down, the vehicle was covered with a tunnel tent of white homespun hemp or linen stretched on hickory bows as a defense against the weather. A good driver so equipped could take fourteen barrels of flour over the five ridges of the Alleghenies and on easier grades could carry two tons. Conestoga wagons and Conestoga draft horses, named from a creek in southeastern Pennsylvania, were probably unsurpassed in the world.

Another stream of humanity consisted of the drovers. As the country increased in size their routes grew longer. By the beginning of the nineteenth century New York City was drawing meat supply from as far north as the Mohawk Valley, and Boston was laying New Hampshire and Vermont under tribute. As early as 1807 Fortescue Cuming passed a drove of a hundred and thirty cattle in Ohio being driven from near Lexington, Kentucky, to Baltimore. Droves of horses and mules moved from the same state to the seaboard South. Mules were in special demand there because they could stand hot weather and the neglect and ill treatment incident to the slavery régime, and, being an infertile stock, they had to be constantly replenished. They were also bred in New York and New England for the Southern market. Though hogs and sheep were driven in large numbers, beef was the main commodity transported on the hoof. Like peddlers, drovers had a name for sharpness. Buyers sometimes lied outrageously about the price of meat, worried the farmers into sales at twenty per cent below the market and then cheated the city butcher at the other end. Daniel Drew began his fortune, tradition says, through discovering new tricks even in that trade. The night before he reached the city he salted his cattle well and then, just before entering, gave the thirsty beasts all the water they could drink. The water cost him nothing, but a full-grown beef could drink some fifty pounds of it, each of which on the butcher's scales brought an added three cents.

Steadily increasing traffic dramatized the need for better highways. The science of road making, neglected since the Romans, was now being redeveloped by Trésaguet in France and by Telford, Metcalf, and Macadam in Great Britain. Naturally, imitative enterprise was stirred in America where such improvements were so vitally needed. New York in 1784 was the first state to aid in the maintenance of local roads, but the small sum voted had little importance save as indicating a new policy. Pennsylvania the following year appropriated two thousand pounds toward building the road from Cumberland County into Pittsburgh. In this and similar undertakings soon thereafter the legislature made state officials responsible for construction and maintenance, though in other instances it placed funds with county commissions to forward local enterprises. New York in 1796 undertook a state-wide policy on similar principles, and the next year it organized a public lottery in order to provide additional funds. Virginia and Maryland, after 1785, inaugurated the expedient of collecting maintenance costs from the users themselves by means of fees paid at pole gates, hinged or pivoted at the roadside and hence known as turnpikes.

English precedent, reënforced by the prevalent zest for speculation, suggested that public good could be joined with private gain by forming road corporations which,

as their profits were to come from tolls, were called turnpike companies. When the first such charter was granted
in 1792 to a company engaging to build a sixty-two
mile highway from Philadelphia to Lancaster, its stock
was immediately oversubscribed. Within two years it
constructed, at seventy-five hundred dollars a mile, a
road declared to be a "masterpiece of its kind . . . paved
with stone the whole way and overlaid with gravel, so
that it is never obstructed during the most severe season."
This success inspired the formation of many other companies, notably in New England. Because of financial
difficulties no other turnpike was built in the Middle
States during the eighteenth century. Nevertheless, by
1821 Pennsylvania had authorized a hundred and forty-
six turnpike concerns and New York companies had
built four thousand miles. A glance at the road map of
Massachusetts reveals why Boston was coming to be
called "the Hub"; but Baltimore was surpassing it and
had become the third city of the Union by 1825 largely
by reason of the seven trunk turnpikes which fed its
trade. Farther to the south only one important turnpike
was built, a state enterprise from Charleston to Columbia, on which South Carolina expended a hundred thousand dollars between 1823 and 1828 besides the proceeds
of the tollgates set up as fast as portions were completed.

The earliest companies were usually granted their
privileges in perpetuity, but later charters specified definite terms. New York provided that a road should
revert to the state as soon as the company recovered its
investment and was realizing an annual profit of fourteen per cent, but apparently no turnpike ever earned so

splendid a return. To induce subscriptions, chartered companies were protected against direct competition. The toll rates, sometimes fixed by statute but generally left to the discretion of the directors, ran from three cents a dozen for driven sheep or swine up to twenty-five cents for a four-wheeled carriage. In most instances a company took over the improvement and maintenance of an existing highway. In laying out a new one it was given the right of eminent domain in buying land and even necessary materials.

The provision in the Ohio enabling act requiring that a twentieth of the proceeds from its federal land sales be appropriated toward constructing roads had immediate effect and served for a time as a precedent with other new Western states. In 1808 Secretary Albert Gallatin, taking a national view of the problem, submitted to Congress a report contemplating a vast federal expenditure of sixteen million dollars, but circumstances, including the War of 1812 and the constitutional scruples of two presidents, prevented the achievement of this grandiose design. The most notable federal enterprise was the Cumberland Road, starting westward in 1810 from the town of that name in Maryland. With a turnpike road to Baltimore, built by private capital, it was known as the National Road or, familiarly, the Old Pike.

The construction of this artery worked miracles in the fortunate towns included on its route. For example, Wheeling, Virginia, had been a straggling, discouraged little settlement isolated on a cliff, but a decade after the Old Pike reached the Ohio it became an important market, with brick buildings and paved streets. The running time to Baltimore was cut from eight to four days, and before long six-horse teams, their harness proudly decked with rings, balls, rosettes, and plumes, were hauling five-ton loads into its warehouses. It was natural that less favored towns should be envious. Pittsburgh feared that it would lose its Eastern trade. But the Pittsburgh "pike" was constantly improved to meet this competition, and gloomy prophecies were not realized.

Lengthening turnpikes accentuated the need for strongly built bridges. While there had been bridges since the seventeenth-century settlements, they were few, short, and none too sound. A tree skillfully felled across a narrow stream might afford the traveler a precarious passage while he swam his horse at the side. Cart bridges, like those the English poet Thomas Moore described in Virginia,

> Made of a few uneasy planks
> In open ranks
> Over rivers of mud,

added excitement to a journey. In the older regions stone arches could occasionally be found, but despite their greater safety they required more capital than most rural communities had to spare. There were no immense American structures like those which John Rennie and "Pontifex Maximus" Telford were building in Great Britain until the construction of the Rochester aqueduct on the Erie Canal in the eighteen-twenties.

Wood, being cheap and plentiful, was used for extensive bridges, especially after the success of the one from Boston to Charlestown, which replaced the ancient ferry in 1785. Seven years later the West Boston bridge was likewise built with pile piers, and others followed, the most famous being that across Lake Cayuga, measuring a mile in length and completed in the first years of the nineteenth century. But the pile bridge, like the conventional row of masonry arches, did not always meet American conditions; those who guided lumber rafts or broad-beamed barges wanted as few piers as possible to impede the way, and wooden piers, when numerous, dammed up the spring ice floes.

To meet these needs the wooden truss bridge was invented, the first important one being that finished in 1792 by Colonel Ewel Hale at Bellows Falls, Vermont, with two spans of a hundred and seventy-five feet each, resting on an island. During the years 1801–1805 Timothy Palmer placed the "permanent bridge" over the Schuylkill at Philadelphia at a cost of three hundred thousand dollars, and a little above it Lewis Wernwag, a young German-American, built the "colossus of Fairmount," whose single arch of three hundred and forty feet was never surpassed in a wooden road bridge. This type carried the weight to the ends of a truss of arches and angles, a principle which, though once known to Leonardo da Vinci and Palladio, was independently discovered by these self-taught American engineers. In 1821 Ithiel Town, a Connecticut architect, published a description of a new kind of bridge, held up along each side by a lattice of planks. Since timbers left exposed would quickly weather and decay, builders obviated this by roofing them like a long barn. Soon the covered bridge became a familiar sight in most Northern valleys.

Frequently bridges, like turnpikes, were financed by companies. Seventy such corporations had already been organized by 1800.

One great enterprise furthered by better roads and bridges was stagecoaching. During the first quarter of the nineteenth century it rose to its climax, thanks largely to the leadership of Levi Pease, a blacksmith of Shrewsbury, Massachusetts. Profiting by the knowledge of roads and horses gained as a military messenger during the Revolutionary War, Captain Pease began a passenger service which he was determined would surpass current standards. With courageous borrowing, ingenuity, and zeal, he and a young partner accumulated sufficient rolling stock, four-horse teams and harness, and in 1783 undertook a through passage from Boston to Hartford, lasting from Monday to Thursday, with a branch line, served by a hired driver, leading to New Haven and the New York boat within another day. During the first months many a trip was made without a passenger, but Pease's persistence was rewarded, and with another partner the route was put through to New York, forming thus the longest and most reliable link in a chain of stages reaching to Richmond in Virginia. Two years later he obtained the first mail contract of this kind granted by the Confederation government, a trust which was to give stagecoaching more prestige and an income upon which it could rely.

As with railroads in a later generation, rivalries brought reckless cutting of fares and eventual combination of lines, especially in eastern New England. The Eastern Stage Coach Company, for example, was chartered in 1818 to operate north from Boston. Within twenty years it was interlocked with turnpike, bridge and bank companies and was paying dividends of ten or eleven per cent. In such incorporations maximum fares were generally set at five cents a mile and the public interest was otherwise protected.

Service was extended rapidly to care for increasing traffic. Stages also penetrated the South, where the dearth of towns and the prevalence of water travel had earlier deterred them. One main route connected at Petersburg, Virginia, with the northern lines, and continued down the piedmont till it branched to Charleston, Savannah, and finally to Montgomery, where river passage could be taken for Mobile. Another went up the Shenandoah Valley and into Tennessee. An Indiana newspaper rejoiced to announce in September, 1820, that a line of stages had been established to run from Louisville through Vincennes to St. Louis. In 1825 appeared the first guidebook of national scope for the benefit of stagecoach travelers, and also the first paper devoted chiefly to stagecoach news.

The growth of communication is most strikingly illustrated by the development of the post office. When the new federal government took charge, the main post route extended from Maine to Georgia, serving fifty offices, with lateral branches reaching half as many more. Vermont, Kentucky, and Tennessee were still untouched, and the line to Pittsburgh, just inaugurated, was the farthest venture into the West. Since the government wanted to make considerable profit from the service, postage was high—it cost thirty-four cents to send a letter from New York to Savannah. At such rates, and especially as most letters were sent postage collect, correspondents made their messages as substantial and readable as possible. It was cheaper, and in many places necessary, to confide a letter to a friendly traveler or a wagoner, but this suffered from the disadvantage that the bearer might feel at liberty to unfold the paper and examine its contents and, if interesting, read it aloud at tavern firesides.

In the 1790's the government, worried by uncertainties as to the loyalty of the trans-Allegheny folk and realizing the political significance of better communication, forsook the policy of profits, reduced the rates, and pushed the service as fast as possible into the remoter regions. By 1792 an ordinary letter cost from six to twenty-five cents, according to the distance, though slightly upward readjustments later had to be made. In 1796 the post reached the garrison at Fort Niagara; a decade later Postmaster General Gideon Granger announced that he had engaged "two faithful, enterprising, hardy young woodsmen" to carry the mails from Cleveland to Detroit, an arduous commission as it meant traversing the Great Black Swamp that stretched from Sandusky Bay to the Maumee River. There was an office at Memphis in 1800 and one at Natchez in 1801. As late as 1825 it was reported that half the mails were transported by horse and rider. The office in the wilderness might be a settler's cabin, but even in the East the postmaster was seldom fully differentiated, usually giving out the mail from a corner in his general store or tavern or printing office. By 1830 the first postmaster general to sit in the President's cabinet could report eight thousand offices and a hundred and fifteen thousand miles of routes, the longest reaching the Rockies.

The stagecoach business was closely related not only to the post office but also in many places to the tavern. While stage men often found it expedient to acquire inns, landlords occasionally branched into staging, even in its early days. The tavern, of course, was more than an adjunct to the stagecoach lines. It had existed long before the advent of wheeled traffic and was to persist after coaches had been laid away in the museums. Yet it was never more lively or more interesting than in the great days of the turnpike. Lodging under its roof the traveler had an opportunity to survey its full activity. In the spacious taproom, especially on court day or during militia muster or a season of land sales, a thirsty multitude would crowd around the bar in the corner. From behind a grating would be served the strong staples —whisky, brandy, gin, and rum—or an outrageous New England drink called "black strap." A party might call for a bowl of American flip, made up of strong beer with a dark rum into which a white-hot iron had been thrust to give it the desired burnt-bitter taste and then poured into mammoth glasses. Toddy and punch could likewise be concocted on demand, while simpler tastes were satisfied with hard cider. But the taproom also sheltered other interests. If the traveler wished to write a letter, he had to use the same rough desk on which the host would calculate his morning's bill. If he sought diversion, and did not care for the juggler or the dancing bear performing in the stable yard, there were draughts, cards, the newspaper, or, best of all, conversation around the mighty fire, where many a yarn was spun, though not always in the stately phrase of Longfellow's *Tales of a Wayside Inn*. On a favored night an attraction might be found in the upstairs long room, perhaps a group of strolling players, a lecture on the elements of science, a party caucus or a dance, when the spring floor, resting on shallow-arch trusses, throbbed with gaiety.

Over all this animated scene presided the landlord, a man of consequence—a "topping man," as the Yankee phrase went—for no one in those days, when the temperance movement was just beginning, thought of bracketing publicans with sinners. The military officer, returning from the Revolution to readjust himself to civil life and noting the increase of traffic, oftentimes decided to capitalize his prestige by taverning. Europeans were astonished to be told that they could breakfast at Major Todd's and dine at Colonel Brown's, but they soon became familiar with this phenomenon of civil and political equality. Owning a good-sized farm and possibly a mill or a distillery in addition to his inn, the landlord was the economic peer of most of his patrons. His daughter waited table without sacrifice of caste and would have been no less surprised than offended had a tip been offered. He himself sat down with his guests. Fenimore Cooper declared that,

The inn-keeper of Old England, and the inn-keeper of New-England, form the very extremes of their class. The one is obsequious to the rich, the other unmoved, and often apparently cold. The first seems to calculate, at a glance, the amount of profit you are likely to leave behind you; while his opposite appears only to calculate in what manner he can most contribute to your comfort, without materially impairing his own. . . . . He is often a magistrate, the chief of a battalion of militia, or even a member of a state legislature.

In taverns, however, as in most other respects, standards varied with the distance from the port towns. There were special sectional differences, too, as among the Pennsylvania Germans, where the stranger found an unfamiliar cuisine. Some, like the Moravians who kept the Sun at Bethlehem, were famous bonifaces. The rougher country inns of that region impressed the traveler with their cleanliness, but the absence of sheets between the feather ticks was deplored. South of the Potomac inns were rare. Where they were good, as the Eagle Tavern at Richmond, the prices were accounted high, though, here as everywhere, lodging was cheaper than food, and could be had in the 1790's for less than thirty cents. But generally they were not good, often a solitary cabin beside a ferry. A traveler of good address, however, could usually find ample entertainment at a planter's house. "Hospitality," wrote Dr. Thomas Cooper in 1794, "is relative: from Massachusetts to Maryland, inns are plenty, and strangers frequent them when they travel: from the south boundary of Pennsylvania to South Carolina, taverns are more scarce and dear, and hospitality is on the most liberal scale." The same observation could have been made through the next forty years. If one found entry to a house, he might leave with a letter to a friend or relative of his host living a day's journey further on, where he would find a welcome from the servants even if the family itself chanced to be

away. A traveler with his store of news relieved the lone-
liness of plantation life.

It is a far cry from the frontier tavern-hut to the
urban caravansaries just beginning to develop in 1790.
The word "hotel," with its suggestion of French luxury,
was apparently first used in America that year. Certainly
the City Hotel, opened four years later in New York,
far outdid any existing hostelry. It had seventy-three
rooms, whereas few others had more than thirty; it was
financed by a stock company; and on both accounts had
somewhat less the atmosphere of personal hospitality. In
1804 the Exchange Coffee House was begun in Boston,
seven stories in height, and in 1807 a similar large-scale
establishment with the same name opened in Philadelphia.
Others soon followed in Baltimore and later in Washington. At the earlier taverns it had been the habit of
bachelors who lived nearby to take their board, a practice
which surprised Europeans. Now, with these enlarged
facilities, whole families took up hotel life, engaging
rooms by the month, if not the year.

But these places were hardly more than oversized inns.
At the very end of the period, in 1829, came something
as new in spirit as it was in aspect—the first-class American hotel, the Tremont House in Boston. Not only was
it the largest in the world, with a hundred and seventy
bedrooms, a granite façade with Doric portico, and ten
large public rooms with marble floors, but the whole
physical arrangement was different. Gone was the swing-
ing sign; the horse yard had changed into a flower
garden; the public rooms were lighted with gas; and
there was running water in the kitchen. Instead of the

dinner being put on all at once, it was served *à la France* in courses. The barroom was set off by itself, and the "office" with the room clerk's desk and stately stairway, the forerunner of the lobby, made its initial appearance. Every door had a patent lock with a special key; washbowl and pitcher stood by every bedside, and soap was furnished free though not yet renewed for each arriving guest; "rotunda men" answered calls from the annunciator connected with each room. Service was the watchword, but still without loss of dignity. It was obviously a place for the rich and the successful; at last democracy had its palace, where the poor might look if not linger. It was, moreover, in almost every feature a characteristically and peculiarly American institution.

Reprinted with permission from John Allen Krout and Dixon Ryan Fox, THE COMPLETION OF INDEPENDENCE *(New York, Macmillan, 1944), A History of American Life, v. 5.*

Some Reflections
on the Rise
of American Sport

T W O years before the Pilgrims, heartened by the example of the Jamestown colonists, sailed out of Plymouth
for some new Plymouth across the sea, there passed under
the royal seal a proclamation of James I touching upon
the lawful sports to be enjoyed by his loyal subjects.
Through the precise phrasing of its pages one gets
glimpses of the religious dissension then stirring England
and the bearing of the dispute upon the traditional pastimes of the populace. The king had discovered in Lanca-
shire and other parts of his kingdom "much discontent
in consequence of the people being deprived of recreation
on Sundays." For this situation he blamed the Puritans
and other austere folk. With the hope of winning popular
support for the Established Church, he ordered that all
who attended services on Sundays and holy days should
be permitted to engage in lawful recreations after worship. In the list of approved sports appear the diversions
of the English countryside: dancing on the green, the
festival around the May-pole, leaping, vaulting, wrestling,
pitching the bar and throwing the sledge, which had

formerly received the sanction of Queen Elizabeth. Archery, encouraged since the days when the longbowman was an important element in England's defense, was not forgotten, while bull-baiting and bear-baiting received a qualified endorsement.

The English villagers and townspeople who followed in the wake of the *Mayflower* and *Sarah Constant* brought to the New World the sports and pastimes with which they had been familiar in the Old, modifying or adding to them as frontier conditions afforded opportunity. They also brought, especially in the case of the settlers along the shores of Massachusetts Bay and in the Connecticut valley, certain prejudices against the popular recreations of the mother country. For them the beauty of the May festival was overshadowed by the fear of inadvertently drifting into a pagan idolatry. Dancing, running, jumping, and kindred sports of the village green were associated in their minds with profanation of the Lord's Day. Animal-baiting and cock-fighting they frowned upon as temptations to idleness and dissolute living. Later commentators, prone to select that which they regarded as unusual and abnormal, have stressed the prejudices and taken the pastimes for granted. They have merrily repeated Macaulay's famous quip that bear-baiting was banned not because it gave pain to the bear but because it gave pleasure to the spectators. They have lamented with Nathaniel Hawthorne the shortcomings of social life in a day when youth regarded the midweek lecture and the subsequent public punishment of felons and criminals as a pleasing treat. They have taught generations of American school children to distinguish between the sad-visaged New Englander moving with sober decorum through a dull routine of work, and the carefree Virginian reveling in the sports of turf and field. Within recent years many historians have insisted that this time-honored distinction between Cavalier and Puritan is less real than apparent, since nowhere in colonial America was there time or opportunity for the development of organized play.

Are we to assume, then, that because games, sports, and other recreations were not highly organized by the early settlers the play impulse was either lacking or carefully suppressed out of deference to Puritan prejudice? Were the colonists really too busy conquering the forces of nature, establishing hearthstone and farmstead, to enjoy the wilderness to which they had come? Everywhere conditioning their activities was the forest. Within its shadow was much that lured as well as repelled. The very trees, which concealed a furtive foe, supplied timbers for the home; the haunts of dangerous beast and troublesome marauder were the source of food and furs. As the pioneer mastered the intricacies of a strange woodcraft, he came to realize the possibilities for the hunter in this boundless woodland. Here was a vast game preserve where no keen-eyed warden earned his living by detecting poachers. No distinction of rank or property determined who should enjoy the privilege of sport with rod and gun. Many a colonist, striving to fill the family larder and replenish the family wardrobe, must have found recreation as well as labor in the enterprise. With John Fenwick he could exclaim: "How prodigal hath nature been to furnish this country with all sorts of wild beast and fowl, which every one hath an interest in and may hunt at his pleasure; where, besides the pleasure in hunting, he may furnish his house with excellent fat venison, turkies, geese, heath-hens, cranes, ducks, and pigeons; and wearied with that he may go a-fishing, where the rivers are so furnished that he may supply himself with fish before he can leave off the recreation."

This close association of work and play was characteristic of the evolution of fun among a people whose lives were spent in the open. As we look back upon the settlements of farmers and seamen, unfamiliar with the restrictions of indoor life, it is difficult to distinguish where necessary industry ended and pleasurable diversion began. Hunting, for example, was an important means of securing a livelihood, but at the same time it afforded individual recreation and cooperative sport. The thrill of luring the wary trout or playing the gamy salmon was not entirely dissipated by the fact that the fisherman thereby earned a part of his subsistence. Mingled with irksome responsibility and constant danger there were delights of sailing for the seaman. From his vocation he derived the joys which the modern yachtsman associates with a diverting avocation: the satisfaction of controlling the force of wind and wave, of compelling the elements to do his bidding, or, if they served him ill, of finding a means to meet the emergency. In similar fashion the routine tasks of the countryside yielded their measure of fun. On each successive frontier barn-raisings, log-rollings, plowing-bees, and corn-huskings were cooperative ventures, which developed into sporting tests of strength and skill so dear to the heart of the pioneer. In them were nurtured the elements of competition and cooperation essential to the success of modern team play. Along the frontier the out-of-door life of the eighteenth century persisted into the nineteenth. In the older communities, however, the opening years of the new century brought a significant change. The clanking of machines was heard; factories arose to house new mechanical devices; steam began to replace water power in operating the machines. Industrialism had come, and the young nation was groping along the path toward economic self-sufficiency. With industry came the large city, thousands of factory hands and office workers crowded indoors that they might be near the source of employment. To an increasing proportion of Americans the out of doors became a memory of youthful pleasures, now too costly to be enjoyed.

By the middle of the century the less desirable effects of this urban environment were sufficiently apparent to arouse public protests. Just seventy years ago this month Oliver Wendell Holmes sagely viewing the situation in the Back Bay section of Boston, sounded a note of warning in the *Atlantic Monthly.* "I am satisfied," he wrote, "that such a set of black-coated, stiff-jointed, soft-muscled, paste-complexioned youth as we can boast in our Atlantic cities never before sprang from loins of Anglo-Saxon lineage. . . . We have a few good boatmen, no good horsemen that I hear of, nothing remarkable, I believe, in cricketing, and as for any great athletic feat performed by a gentleman in these latitudes, society would drop a man who should run around the Common in five minutes." A few years earlier the English angler and nimrod, Henry William Herbert, better known by his pen name of Frank Forester, had lamented the fact that Americans scarcely knew the meaning of the word sportsman, since in most communities they reserved the appellation for one who consistently bet on the races or by the light of the flickering lamp watched expectantly the green field of the gaming table. In 1856, Edward Everett, who was not unfamiliar with collegiate circles, deplored the failure of his countrymen to give attention to "manly outdoor exercises which strengthen the mind by strengthening the body."

Perhaps these jeremiads somewhat overstated the case. Certainly, their authors were not able to foresee the remarkable change already in its initial stages. The very forces of industrialization and urbanization which had placed many Americans within the restrictive limits of indoor life ultimately enabled them to rediscover the out of doors and to substitute for a vanishing frontier a system of highly organized sports as a safety valve in a strenuous age. By the decade of the sixties the accumulation of wealth in our rapidly growing cities offered to a part of the urban population a chance to escape from an environment far from attractive. At the same time the developing lines of railroad and steamship transportation rendered mountain lakes, woodland streams, and stretches of seacoast easily accessible. For some this meant a country home and the return to a life in the open during at least part of the year. Others sought watering places or mountain resorts, where they built pretentious villas or rented small cottages, as the crowds at the hotels and boarding houses became too large and heterogeneous. In the hour of high spirits which followed Vicksburg and Gettysburg, William R. Travers and his associates opened a new race course at Saratoga and profited handsomely from the liberal patronage of New York's fashionable set. At the close of the war Newport could scarcely accommodate the summer visitors, while many followed President Grant to Long Branch, when he made the New Jersey resort the nation's summer capital. Shrewd investors quickly exploited the choice spots of the Adirondacks and White Mountains. Nor was distance a deterrent to those seeking an interesting vacation. Scarcely had the battle shouts of the Indians died away in Colorado before Denver, Davos, and Colorado Springs had become rendezvous for tourists. In the South, Jacksonville, Florida, was a mecca for pleasure seekers, its population doubling every winter season in the decade of the seventies.

Although an increasing number of nonmanual workers were enjoying what had formerly been a luxury—an annual vacation—the great majority of city dwellers could not seek recreation far afield. For them outdoor sports and games offered relief from the strain and nervous tension of a hurried life. Unlike the earlier generations of Americans, they did not associate their play with their work, but they carried into it that genius for systematic organization which had become an outstanding characteristic of expanding industry. With bewildering rapidity teams were formed and federated into national associations. Local clubs became mere units in leagues which recognized the jurisdiction of a governing body clothed with sweeping control of methods and principles. It was indeed the heyday of *organized* sport.

Prominent in the list of athletic activities was baseball. Developing out of such games as "four-old-cat," rounders, and town ball in the decade after 1830, it possessed elements ancient in origin and known to peoples in many lands. Among the exhibits in the British Museum is a leather-covered ball more than thirty centuries old, stuffed with papyrus waste, its segments of cover sewn in such a way as to make it appear an ancestor of the modern baseball. In the long span of years since that ball was used in the valley of the Nile mankind has found many ways of playing ball, but the English seem to have been the first to invent a game in which the bat was used to score runs and thus determine the issue of the contest. Their stool-ball, rounders, and cricket were finally supplanted in this country by a type of baseball perfected through the ingenuity of Abner Doubleday at Cooperstown, New York, in 1839. The Doubleday style of play grew in favor so rapidly that by 1860 there was an association of baseball clubs in the northeastern states. Although the Civil War temporarily checked the formation of new teams, it brought potential nines together in the camps and behind the battle lines, where it served as an escape from the realities of the battlefield. The intersectional movements of the armies tended to make the sport national, for soldiers can carry more than shelterhalfs and condiment cans in their knapsacks. Following the war came a change in the status of the player, when the Cincinnati Red Stockings, the first professional club, demonstrated in 1869 the possibility of organizing the game on sound business principles. Within two years the professional ball players had a national association. The amateur, however, persisted. He converted vacant lots and school grounds into playing fields, while the professional groped his way toward the formation of the National League in 1876, which has remained the senior circuit of organized baseball ever since.

During the decade of the seventies, years of importance in the expansion of baseball, there were innumerable manifestations of the rise of sport. At Jerome Park in Westchester County, New York, where Leonard W. Jerome, William R. Travers, and August Belmont were trying to redeem the reputation of the turf, the well-appointed carriages in which the wealthy residents of Murray Hill had driven out across the Harlem indicated that the social dictators of the metropolis had smiled upon the venture. On a glorious May day in 1875, the Kentucky Derby was first run at Churchill Downs and immediately became a national event for three-year-olds. On the road as well as the turf amateur reinsmen engaged in tests of speed. In the halcyon days of prosperity which marked the nation's recovery from the panic of 1873, few of the rising captains of industry were without a pair of fast trotters and correctly appointed road wagon, prepared to engage in spirited brushes on the road. Their example was followed throughout the country by all who could afford to imitate, even in plebeian fashion, the patricians of the highways.

More strenuous than the stimulating sports of horsemanship were the games and exercises sponsored by the urban athletic clubs. Foremost among them both in point of time and influence was the New York Athletic Club, which three years after its formation secured a tract of land north of the Harlem River at Mott Haven, where it constructed in 1871 the first cinder track in the country and opened its games to all athletes who could qualify as amateurs. The program of events was not elaborate, including the 100-yard dash, the half-mile, mile, and three-mile runs, and the three-mile walk, but the invitation to all amateurs sounded a new note amidst the highly commercialized activities of professional runners and pedestrians. So successful was the New York club that it was soon imitated in most of the large cities, the early groups being truly devoted to a regime of physical exercise rather than to the social ventures of wealthy sportsmen. As a result of their rapidly permeating influence there came a demand for definition of amateur status and supervision of track and field meets. Accordingly, the National Association of Amateur Athletes of America undertook the task in 1879, continuing its control until superseded by the Amateur Athletic Union nine years later.

The games of the New York Athletic Club at Mott Haven were a powerful factor in arousing the college student from his lethargy. Within a year Yale staged the first intercollegiate field meet, while in 1874 ten eastern schools participated in the track events which served as a prelude for the rowing regatta at Saratoga. Two years later the Intercollegiate Athletic Association was formed and the long campaign to establish records had begun. In fact the colleges turned to athletics with such abandon that contemporary cartoonists changed their caricature of the undergraduate, as a hollow-chested creature "all brains and no physique," to that of a muscular paragon bereft of all intelligence.

On eastern campuses interest in intercollegiate competition increased. Rowing regattas, which had been sporadic events since a race on Lake Winnipesaukee between Harvard and Yale in 1852, were held with regularity after the formation of the Rowing Association of American Colleges in 1870. At times sixteen or seventeen crews covered the three-mile straightaway course on the Connecticut at Springfield, or on the lake at Saratoga. In 1878 Harvard and Yale began their historic series on the Thames at New London, with the cheers of thousands of supporters urging them to their utmost endeavor. During the same year a Columbia crew returned to receive a tremendous ovation for its victories over both Oxford and Cambridge on the English Thames.

Meanwhile football, though eclipsed by baseball, was taking its place as a campus sport. Princeton and Rutgers had experimented with a form of the English Association game as early as 1869, but the twenty-five players on each side were bewildered by the indefinite character of the rules. A notice in the Harvard *Magenta* for 1874 announced that "the McGill University Football Club will meet the Harvard Club on Jarvis Field, May 14 and 15. The game probably will be called at three o'clock. Admittance 50 cents. The proceeds will be devoted to the entertainment of our visitors from Montreal." Thus Americans were introduced to the novel feature of running with the ball, which had been worked out by the English schoolboys at Rugby. So favorable was the impression made by the rugby game that the Harvard paper recommended that it be substituted for the "somewhat sleepy game now played by our men." The next year Yale agreed to meet Harvard under "concessionary rules" based on the Rugby code, and in 1876 representativies of Princeton, Columbia, Yale, and Harvard, meeting in the Massasoit House in Springfield, Massachusetts, formed the Intercollegiate Football Association. The English rugby game had become American.

Outside collegiate circles, also, the attitude toward outdoor recreation had definitely changed. Croquet, introduced from England with the highest references in 1866, swept over the country like an epidemic. Scythe and sickle prepared lawns and vacant lots for expensive English sets of balls and mallets, while the new home was not complete unless a smooth expanse of grass was set apart for the game. It enticed all ages into the open air. It began the process, later accelerated by archery, tennis, and bicycling, of bringing the women out of stuffy living rooms and parlors to participate in outdoor exercise with men. On many a shady lawn, where a group of iron statuary bespoke the financial status of the household, croquet offered to vivacious girls and demure young women a mild transition from the restrictions which had hemmed in their mothers to that greater freedom which their daughters were destined to enjoy.

While the experts were converting croquet into a game as scientific as billiards and organizing a national association which supervised annual tournaments, two young men at Nahant, Massachusetts, were initiating their friends into the mysteries of sphairistike. It had been adapted in the summer of 1873 by Major Walter O. Wingfield, of the British Army, from a medieval French game. Dr. James Dwight, touring in England the following year, mastered its principles and taught his friend Richard D. Sears. The two introduced the sport at Newport in 1875, the very year that it was christened by its English devotees, lawn tennis. For several years players did not take seriously the diversion of batting a ball back and forth over a net, but in 1881 the United States Lawn Tennis Association had established the sport on such a reputable basis that even the crowd at the Newport Casino was duly impressed.

While tennis was winning its hundreds, the bicycle was affording excitement and amusement to thousands. At the Centennial Exposition in Philadelphia a small display of English-made machines had aroused interested comment. Some had listed them as another foolish fad from abroad; others had recalled with grim smiles their previous failure to master the velocipede; while a few had been impressed by the improvements of the new wheel over the old wooden "bone-shaker." The bicycle in 1876 possessed a high front wheel to which were attached crank-like pedals and a small rear wheel scarcely eighteen inches high, each equipped with a solid rubber tire. The wheels were connected by a curved backbone surmounted by a none too soft saddle from which the rider carefully steered the machine, for the smallest obstacle might mean a dive over the handlebars. It was a device to try men's souls, yet bold young blades practiced secretly in barns and abandoned warehouses, promptly becoming patrons of the dispensers of arnica and court plaster. In the end perseverance triumphed and the high wheel became a delightful, though somewhat precarious, resource for open-air recreation. By 1880 the League of American Wheelmen with several thousand members had inaugurated a series of annual meets which drew expert cyclists from every section of the nation.

More than half a century has elapsed since organized sport in its protean forms thus captured the imagination of the country. With the passing years we have manifested an ever-increasing interest, until our attitude has become somewhat akin to veneration. It may not be heresy, however, even in this season when we worship at the shrines of American football, to ask whether modern sport has merited the praise and attention which we lavish upon it. To its credit much may be counted. It has afforded large numbers of urban dwellers, possessed of considerable leisure, many opportunities to escape the restriction of sedentary life. It has provided a valuable substitute for that social safety valve which was the American frontier. On many a hard-fought field it has kept a flag of idealism flying, which was sorely needed in the frankly opportunistic ethics of the modern business world. It has dotted the land with ball parks and concrete stadia wherein are staged spectacles more regal than those of ancient Rome. It has given us a company of skilled athletes in each generation well worthy of emulation. But organized sport has had its muckers as well as its heroes. Into the spontaneous exuberance of play it has carried much of the shrewd calculation of the horse trade. It has made of intercollegiate football not a game but a vast machine, which threatens by its very complexity to defeat the reason for its being. It has not made us a nation of participants in sports, but a nation of spectators at sporting events. Millions of us still take our outdoor exercise vicariously. By reading the sporting page we attach ourselves to the accomplishments of the team. In the bleachers we share in the home runs and the stolen bases. From dizzy heights on autumnal Saturdays we look down upon twenty-two men struggling for supremacy and feel the joy of combat. There may be benefit in all this, but it hardens no muscles and reduces no waist lines. Perhaps it would not be amiss in the coming years if we pondered well the question of whether from the plethora of sports our nation has reaped an adequate harvest.

Reprinted with permission from the PROCEEDINGS *of the Association of History Teachers of the Middle States and Maryland, no. 26:84–93, 1929.*

✕ IV ✻

LOCAL HISTORY

J O H N   K R O U T ' s *interest in localized history has never been antiquarian. In whatever direction he has exercised this interest—the Empire State, the far-ranging projects of the National Park Service, the American History Research Center, the American Association for State and Local History—he has been concerned with it as a microcosm for a better understanding of America at large. On the occasion of the semicentennial of the charter of the City of New York, which bound the present five boroughs into the Greater City, he joined Allan Nevins in preparing a commemorative history. A quarter century earlier, he had written the vignette on Henry Raymond,* Civil War editor of the* New York Times.

Framing the Charter

"'THE sun will rise this morning upon the greatest experiment in municipal government that the world has ever known—the enlarged city. . . . The end of the old New York and the beginning of the greater city were marked last night by perhaps the biggest, noisiest and most hilarious New Year's Eve celebration that Manhattan Island has ever known." Thus did the New York *Tribune* on January 1, 1898, hail the creation of the new metropolis.

The public demonstration in the closing hours of the old year had reached its climax at City Hall. There Hearst's alert associates on the New York *Journal* had appropriately arranged everything for the formal ceremonies, except the weather. A cold rain fell early in the evening, turning to damp snow before midnight. But the big eyes of many a searchlight winked intermittent flashes of daylight over City Hall Park and the surrounding streets. Red and green flares and set pieces of fireworks of every description sent rainbow effects high into the foggy air. Aerial bombs exploded; and a huge balloon trailing skirts of colored flame floated out toward the harbor. By the time the procession of prominent citizens, civic organizations, and singing societies, with a long line of brilliantly illuminated floats, reached the scene, the police were having difficulty maintaining their lines against the throngs along the west side of Broadway and the east side of Park Row. The hundreds of voices in the combined choral societies could scarcely be heard above the shrieking whistles of the tugs and ferry boats in the rivers.

As the hands of the clock moved toward twelve, there was a solemn moment. Mayor Phelan of San Francisco, in his office far across the continent, touched an electric button and the city ensign of Greater New York rose slowly to the top of the flagstaff on City Hall. The chimes of Trinity Church "rang out the old," and the multitude, led by the German singing societies, lifted its voice in "Auld Lang Syne" before the music was overwhelmed in the raucous noise of jubilation.

The reporter who remarked that the flag of Greater New York rose rather unsteadily to the top of the flagstaff may have been thinking about the uncertainties, the difficulties, the bitterness which had marked the struggle to achieve political consolidation. The controversy had been drawn out over many years; and some who had finally supported the idea of union had done so reluctantly, unconvinced that it would solve the problems of municipal government which, as James Bryce had forcefully pointed out, were usually so ineptly handled in America.

It is impossible to determine the origin of the idea that the boundaries of the City of New York should be expanded to include Brooklyn, Long Island City, Staten Island, and the surrounding towns and villages. Brooklynites thought that they had detected Manhattan's expansionist tendencies as early as 1833, when their petition to the state legislature for a municipal charter had been opposed by the Mayor and aldermen of New York on the ground that incorporation of Brooklyn should occur only in connection with New York. After Brooklyn became a city in 1834, little talk of union was heard for twenty years; but by mid-century the developing commerce of the busy harbor created difficulties which could not be quickly resolved by separate political entities. In 1857 Henry C. Murphy, a former Mayor of Brooklyn, who was to be President Buchanan's Minister to the Netherlands, spoke for many discerning businessmen when he said: "It requires no spirit of prophecy to foretell the union of New York and Brooklyn at no distant day. The river which divides them will soon cease to be a line of separation, and, bestrode by the colossus of commerce, will prove a link which will bind them together." In 1874, New York annexed three townships— Kingsbridge, West Farms, and Morrisania—lying west of the Bronx River in Westchester County.

For more than forty years, however, Greater New York was but an idea in men's minds. That it finally became reality was primarily the result of the intelligent and persistent activity of one man—Andrew Haswell Green. His was that unselfish devotion to high ideals which has ever marked the true reformer. While a member of the New York Park Board in 1868, he became convinced that any system of public improvements, to be successful, would have to be supported by the whole metropolitan district. That, he insisted, meant the political integration of the territory surrounding the City of New

York into a great municipality. So steadfastly did he present his arguments that the plan for consolidation became known as "Green's hobby"; but the singleness of purpose which the term implied was not marred by any hint of folly.

Although Andrew H. Green liked to point out that the lines of unity had been laid down by nature when it "grouped together in close indissoluble relation, at the mouth of a great river, our three islands, Manhattan, Long and Staten, making them buttresses and breakwaters of a capacious harbor," he was quite unwilling to wait patiently for nature to take its course. During the seventies and eighties he had strong support in the New York press, and a Municipal Union Society listed the advantages—lower taxes, increased realty values, better municipal services—which would result from the creation of a Greater New York. The legislators at Albany received numerous petitions and gave serious consideration to several bills which would have brought Brooklyn and New York under a common government.

Such opposition as the friends of consolidation encountered came in large measure from Brooklyn. If the construction of the East River Bridge and its opening in 1883 gave new impetus to the demands of New Yorkers for territorial expansion, it produced the opposite effect on Long Island. Brooklyn's leading newspapers, the *Eagle* and the *Standard-Union*, may not have spoken for the majority of their readers, but they were forthright in opposing annexation to New York. "We might have thought of matrimony once," said the *Eagle*, "but now it is out of the question." To this the *Standard-Union*

added: "What New York would do for or with Brooklyn if it had the power can be imagined, and the people
of the latter, without regard to party, do not intend to
try the experiment. They will hold on to their independence and take care of themselves."

Green and his associates realized that this sentiment
could not be dismissed as unreasonable provincialism,
and they redoubled their efforts to persuade their reluctant fellow citizens. With some help from the state
administration, under Governor David B. Hill, they
secured the passage of an act, which the Governor approved on May 8, 1890, creating "a commission to in-
quire into the expediency of consolidating the various
municipalities in the State of New York occupying the
several islands in the harbor of New York." No powerful
opponents of consolidation were named to the Board;
and, with Andrew Green in the chair and J. S. T. Stranahan, a prominent Brooklyn advocate of union as the
vice president, it was not difficult to guess what the final
report would be. The commissioners, having heard testi-
mony on both sides, drafted a bill advocating immediate
creation of a Greater New York.

The legislature, however, moved with caution. It took
almost four years to devise a formula which suited the
majority. Then, in 1894, the consolidationists won their
first major victory. A bill was passed enabling the voters
in the metropolitan district to vote on the question of
consolidation. There were rumors of a "deal" between
Democratic and Republican politicians; but it is more
likely that the lobby in favor of the bill had finally convinced the influential leaders at Albany that a popular

referendum on the subject was politically harmless. However that may be, the proponents of a greater city were ready to seize their opportunity. Arguments often heard in committee room and private conference were now restated to make a wider public appeal. The informal groups which had been working earnestly through the years now sought more effective organization.

By common consent Brooklyn was considered the chief battleground. There, more than on Manhattan Island, the roots of local loyalty had struck deeply, giving strength to those who wanted to preserve the social characteristics of an earlier day. Brooklynites who cherished the image of their city as a small community of homes, schools, and churches, little touched by the urgencies of manufacturing and commerce, were unpersuaded when they heard that metropolitan consolidation would mean more population, greater business opportunities, lower taxes, lower interest on mortgages, increased employment, and more extensive public works. They doubted that the problems of their own municipal government, which were too often mishandled by the political machine, could be solved by adding the problems of another municipality, which had experienced similar difficulties under an even more powerful political machine.

Fortunately for the expansionists, they had the aid of the Consolidation League, an organization which claimed more than 40,000 enrolled voters in 1894. It served in the campaign as a spearhead for the friends of a Greater New York, mobilizing civic reformers, politicians, businessmen, real estate speculators, in a supreme effort to

win the plebiscite. In the end superior organization won
—a narrow victory. Brooklyn cast 64,744 votes in favor
of consolidation and 64,467 against. In other parts of the
metropolitan district the results were more decisive. New
York, Queens, and Richmond counties rolled up a favorable majority of almost 44,000 votes; while the little
towns of Eastchester and Pelham gave 625 in favor and
413 against. The final tabulation for the metropolitan
district showed that consolidation had been favored by
176,170 and rejected by 131,706.

Andrew Green and his enthusiastic colleagues inter-
preted this vote as a mandate to proceed at once with
consolidation. During the weeks following the election
they made sure that they had the support of the incoming
administration of Governor Levi P. Morton. In his first
message to the legislators in January, 1895, Governor
Morton proposed that "a commission be at once created
to be composed of the most capable citizens of the various localities interested, and to be charged with the power
and the duty of framing a charter and reporting the same
to the present legislature."

While the legislature debated the proper terms of such
a bill, popular sentiment against consolidation seemed to
be rising. In New York the election of Mayor William
L. Strong on a reform platform had weakened the support of certain Democratic politicians who had been
favorable; in Brooklyn the closeness of the vote in the
recent referendum had encouraged the opponents of consolidation. The more determined among them formed the
League of Loyal Citizens under the leadership of William
C. Redfield, who was later to become Secretary of Com-

merce in the cabinet of Woodrow Wilson. They soon claimed an active membership of 50,000, established an efficient legislative lobby in Albany, and financed a vigorous publicity campaign to prevent the passage of any consolidation bill.

To Green and Stranahan and their associates, the League and its followers were standing in the way of progress. By refusing to accept the trend of events, they were playing into the hands of professional politicians who hated to lose their power. Loyalty to an independent Brooklyn was curtly dismissed as "a sort of senile sentimentalism that is really quite incapable of appreciating the changes that the lapse of time demands for the development of great thriving communities, and which vainly strives to stay the wheels of beneficent progress."

The influence of the League, however, could not be ignored. It reached as far as Albany, where it was strengthened by the support of residents of New York who had begun to doubt whether such municipal problems as taxation, transportation, fire and police protection, public health and sanitation, parks and public improvements would be brought any nearer solution by extending the boundaries of their city. No one can say how important this opposition was in determining the vote of the legislators. At any rate, when a bill to permit consolidation and to authorize the preparation of a charter for the proposed Greater New York came before the Senate, it was defeated by two votes, with every Senator from Brooklyn and New York City voting in the negative.

Thus, the legislative session of 1895 ended in disap-

pointment for the consolidationists. They had to be content with the passage of an act, known as the Annexation
Bill, which permitted New York to acquire certain additional territory in Westchester County east of the
Bronx River—Throg's Neck, Unionport, Westchester,
Williamsbridge, Bronxdale, Olinville, Baychester, Eastchester, Wakefield, Bartow—bringing the city line north
to Yonkers, Mount Vernon, Pelham, and New Rochelle.
Behind the scenes, however, they were winning influential supporters, none more important than Thomas
C. Platt, "boss" of the state Republican organization. For
many years Platt had been either opposed or indifferent
to consolidation, but by the autumn of 1895 he was ready
to give the proposal his political blessing. The reasons for
his change in attitude are not entirely clear. Probably his
friends were too kind when they attributed his new position to that "patriotic and constructive statesmanship"
which realized that "consolidation was right and logical
and necessary to the complete and rational development
of the metropolis." He may have realized also that the
charter of Greater New York could be framed along
lines reviving the legislative commission system, with the
probability of Republican stalwarts securing the controlling positions.

When Governor Morton reminded the legislature in
1896 that he still desired a law for the consolidation of
the metropolitan area, his words seemed to be in the form
of a command. Every legislator knew that "Boss" Platt
was now openly supporting the proposal, and many had
heard rumors of a "deal" between the Republican state
organization and the leaders of Tammany Hall. A law

was quickly passed authorizing a joint committee of assemblymen and senators to investigate the desirability of extending the boundaries of New York. With Senator Clarence Lexow as chairman, the committee listened to petitions and counter-petitions revealing the division of sentiment in both New York and Brooklyn; and then asked the legislature to create a charter commission and set January 1, 1898, as the date for the establishment of Greater New York.

While this recommendation was making its way—and a stormy way it was—through the State Assembly, the friends and foes of consolidation had renewed their warfare. The lines of division were not hard and fast, for men changed their minds on the subject as they tried to calculate all of its implications. For example, Seth Low, president of Columbia University and long a consolidationist, now joined with former Mayor Abram S. Hewitt, Elihu Root, and other members of the City Club in a petition to the legislature, protesting that the Lexow Bill would force New York to annex territory "that has either been deprived for a long time of local improvements, or has been driven by the peculiarity of its position into a recklessness born of indifference." The *Tribune* warned its readers that consolidation should not be adopted until the details had been carefully worked out and critically examined.

Citizens of New York, who joined the Taxpayers Anti-Equalization League, fearing an increase in their tax bills, were encouraged by the determined resistance to annexation in Brooklyn. President Redfield of the League of Loyal Citizens guided the propaganda and tactics of his organization so adroitly that its members seemed to represent the dominant opinion in their city. They secured more than seventy thousand signatures to a petition requesting the Legislature to resubmit the question to the voters. Theodore B. Willis, leader of the local Republican machine, and Dr. Littlejohn, Episcopal Bishop of Long Island, agreed that Brooklyn had a spirit and tradition of its own which would be destroyed by union with New York.

On the other side, there were also strong forces. The combativeness of Dana's *Sun* and the editorial vigor of Pulitzer's *World* steadily sustained the expansionists. In Brooklyn they had to be content with the support of the *Citizen*, but it was widely read by organization Democrats and by persons active in labor circles. Among businessmen, Stranahan and his associates in the Consolidation League were still influential, and they had now the cooperation of such civic leaders as Lewis M. Peck and William J. Gaynor, who was later to become Mayor of Greater New York.

The decisive factor in the situation was the power of Tom Platt. Without his aid the Lexow Bill would not have passed the Assembly. Even with his unfailing support the bill barely received the necessary votes. When his own lieutenants failed him, Platt turned to Tammany and found there his margin of victory.

Under the State Constitution, as revised in 1894, the mayors of the cities affected by the Lexow Bill had the right to accept or reject it. Since both Mayor Frederick Wurster of Brooklyn and Mayor William L. Strong of New York vetoed the bill, it had to be repassed by the

Legislature. This was no easy task; but again Platt demonstrated his mastery. Many Democrats refused to cooperate further, and the bill became a party measure. In the final roll call only 6 of the 114 Republicans in the Assembly and only one of the 36 Republicans in the Senate voted in the negative. When Andrew H. Green heard that Governor Morton had signed the measure he hurried into Platt's office and said: "I came in to express my gratitude to the Father of Greater New York." To this Platt replied: "And I desire to express my appreciation of the marvelous devotion and work of the Grandfather of Greater New York."

The law of consolidation had been written, but no one knew what the governmental forms of the new metropolis would be. Governor Morton, in May, 1896, appointed a charter commission which inspired popular confidence. Benjamin F. Tracy, who had been Secretary of the Navy under President Harrison, was named president. His associates were: Seth Low, Judge John F. Dillon, and Ashbel P. Fitch from New York; Stewart L. Woodford (who was later named by President McKinley to be Minister at Madrid), Silas B. Dutcher, and William C. Dewitt from Brooklyn; Garret J. Garretson from Queens; and George M. Pinney, Jr., from Richmond. Members *ex officio*, in addition to Mayor Strong of New York and Mayor Wurster of Brooklyn, were Andrew H. Green, Campbell W. Adams, Theodore E. Hancock, and Patrick J. Gleason. A subcommittee on draft, under the chairmanship of William C. Dewitt, began the difficult task of framing a fundamental law for a municipality of more than 3,100,000 persons, living within an area of

359 square miles; for the boundaries of the enlarged city were to include old New York and "all municipal corporations and parts of such corporations, other than counties, within the counties of Kings and Richmond, Long Island City, the towns of Newtown, Flushing and Jamaica and that part of Hempstead in Queens County, west of a line drawn from Flushing between Rockaway Beach and Shelter Island to the Ocean."

The charter commission was able to present its first draft as a "gift to the city" on Christmas morning. A small group of political leaders, including Governor Morton, Governor-elect Frank S. Black, Lieutenant-Governor Timothy C. Woodruff, and "Boss" Platt had celebrated Christmas Eve at Governor Morton's home in New York by expressing approval of the document. The legislature acted promptly, passing the bill in February, 1897. Within a few weeks Brooklyn opinion likewise accepted the charter. If surrender to New York was inevitable, the terms were unexpectedly favorable. Thankful that his earlier fears had been groundless, Mayor Wurster signed away his city's independence.

While Brooklyn rejoiced, New York denounced. Its citizens were suddenly appalled by the magnitude of the new responsibilities which they were assuming. Nothing in the charter lifted their spirits or gave promise of a happier future. Editorial writers in the *Times* and the *Tribune* pointed to confusing provisions and agreed with the Chamber of Commerce that it was difficult to see how the taxpayers of New York could profit under the new government. Ex-Mayor Hewitt and ex-Mayor Grace asked the legislature to give the charter further consideration.

This view was endorsed by the Bar Association, the Real Estate Exchange, the Reform Club, the Union League Club, the City Club, and the Board of Trade and Transportation. E. L. Godkin, still writing incisively for the *Evening Post*, insisted that the charter was apt to reverse the trend toward greater democracy in American municipal government. Beneath the apparent concentration of power in the mayor's office he saw a diffusion of responsibility among boards and commissions. He doubted that effective local self-government would mark the initial years of the enlarged city.

As a member of the charter commission Mayor Strong had agreed to the charter's provisions. As Mayor of New York he sent it back to Albany with his veto and thus forced the legislature to pass it again. This proved to be a mere formality, for the lines in the legislature held, as Platt said they would. Governor Black, performing the service expected of him, signed the charter on May 4, 1897.

Perhaps the strong criticism of the structure of government was a distinct advantage to the citizens of Greater New York. They had read so much concerning the inherent weakness of a federal system resting upon the creation of the five boroughs that they expected difficulties. They had been warned so often of the administrative conflicts which might arise between the various departments and commissions that they were prepared for the necessity of charter revision. Aware of the experimental nature of much of the structure as well as the functioning of their new government, they were pleasantly surprised when it proved far more workable than its critics had been willing to concede. It was possible to fix power as well as responsibility in the office of mayor; and the board of estimate and apportionment developed quickly into a policy-making and finance-controlling body, emphasizing both the autonomy and the federal unity of the boroughs. Most important of all, the charter (the worst imperfections of which were cured by a thorough revision in 1901), provided the opportunity for that "imperial city" which Andrew Green had long prophesied would some day rise above the three islands at the mouth of the "lordly Hudson."

Reprinted with permission from Allan Nevins and John Allen Krout, eds., THE GREATER CITY: NEW YORK, *1898–1948 (New York, Columbia University Press, 1948).*

Henry J. Raymond
on the Republican Caucuses
of July, 1866

E A R L Y in the summer of 1866 relations between the White House and the Capitol had frayed to a breaking point in the bitter controversy over a reconstruction policy. Only a handful of the moderates, who had defended the veto of the Freedmen's Bureau bill in February and had acquiesced in the presidential disapproval of the Civil Rights act the following month, were still on amicable terms with Andrew Johnson. In June Congress threw down the gage of battle by passing with large majorities a proposed amendment to the Constitution, prepared, under the watchful eye of Thaddeus Stevens, by the Joint Committee of Fifteen on Reconstruction. The President accepted the challenge by advising his friends to oppose ratification of the Congressional proposal. The issue then rested with the state legislatures. By the second week in July it had become evident that the constructive work of the Congressional session was rapidly nearing completion, but neither house seemed anxious to decide upon a date for adjournment. In view of the unusual importance of the autumn election this reluctance to leave Washington appeared ominous. Congressmen who normally were eager to repair their political fences between sessions professed an unwonted willingness to remain at their posts of duty, even during the midsummer heat. This apparent devotion to the nation's legislative business was the subject of caustic comment in the press, but the legislators' motives were not fully revealed until the caucus of Union Republican members assembled on the evening of July 11.

Called for the purpose of discussing the proper time for the first session of the Thirty-ninth Congress to adjourn, the caucus developed into a frank, and somewhat acrimonious, exchange of views upon the political reasons for prolonging the session. Though the ban of secrecy had been imposed at the opening of the meeting, the New York *Herald* on the following morning contained a graphic but slightly erroneous account of the proceedings. "Radical Congressional Caucus—Exciting and Significant Scenes—The Radical Dry Bones Rattling" ran the half-inch headlines announcing the disclosures to follow.

Several members took the floor advocating the continuance of the present session until the future policy of the President could be more definitely ascertained or some measures passed limiting the appointing power. The general drift of these speeches was to the effect that inasmuch as many members of the House were anxious to return to their homes and provide for their re-election, that body might adjourn and go home, but that the Senate should not concur and remain in session. It was not considered necessary to retain a quorum of the latter body even, as a less number could adjourn from day to day and thus perpetuate the session and prevent the President from turning out the radical office-holders and appointing conservatives without the advice and consent of the Senate. All agreed that the present office-holders throughout the country must be retained. It would never do to have a new set working against the Republican Party.

The completeness of the *Herald's* report of the caucus surprised Congressmen, until it was discovered that one of James Gordon Bennett's ingenious reporters had gained admission to the press gallery of the House of Representatives by a judicious use of greenbacks on a doorkeeper who had imbibed too freely from the cup that cheers. Ejected before the discussion was finished, the eavesdropper relied upon his imagination to finish off the account. From such a source, then, the newspaper controversy over the actual proceedings of the caucus took its origin. The *Tribune, World, and Times* were filled with charges and countercharges during the week following July 12.

Some new light is shed upon the nature of the caucus of July 11, as well as upon that of July 13, in an unpublished notebook among the papers of Henry J. Raymond. A member of the Thirty-ninth Congress from the sixth New York district, Raymond was regarded by his colleagues as the leader of the Johnson forces on the floor of the House. The New York *Times*, of which he was editor, supported President Johnson on all important questions connected with the political and economic reconstruction of the Southern states. Not only because of the commentator's prestige and influence, but also because his comment bears upon the whole question of the relation of presidential patronage to the dispute between Congress and President Johnson, Mr. Raymond's obviously personal memorandum is of more than ordinary interest. While the account is probably colored by the writer's political affiliations at the moment, it is sufficiently less partisan than the statements which appeared in the *Times* to warrant the belief that it is in the main an accurate record. Under date of July 12, the morning after the first caucus, Mr. Raymond wrote:

A caucus of Republican M.C.'s was held last evening in the hall of the Ho. of Reps. which was of considerable importance as foreshadowing the purpose and plans of the leading Radicals.

On motion of Mr. Morill of Vt., Banks of Mass. was elected Chairman and Mr. Ferry of Mich. Secretary. The caucus, so far as the House was concerned, was quite full but only eight senators were present.

Mr. Hotchkiss of N.Y. said that the meeting was called at the request of himself and others and its object was to have an interchange of views as to the next course to be pursued in regard to the rumored removal of office-holders by the President. He had no doubt that such removal was intended as soon as Congress should adjourn and in his state the "head butcher" had been appointed and stood at the door ready to strike. He deemed it the duty of Congress to stand by its friends and to make any sacrifice necessary to keep them in office. He thought Congress should remain in session so as to prevent removals.

A motion was put and carried that no member should speak more than five minutes nor more than once. Mr. Cobb of Wisconsin offered a resolution declaring every one present to be in honor bound to act in Congress and out in accordance with the decision of the caucus,—but this was voted down: a resolution of secrecy was adopted.

Mr. Farnsworth of Illinois then offered a resolution declaring that Congress would remain in session until December. He said any party that did not stand by its friends ought to go down, and we must stand by the men now in office. He thought it might be necessary for Congress to take other action before next session to prevent the accomplishment of schemes to restore the rebels to power. He believed the President was a traitor to the party and to the country and that he was ready for any measure, however desperate, which would put the govt. into the hands of the rebels. What his schemes were he did not know, but he had been told on good authority that Mr. Seward had said that this Congress would not meet again until the Southern States were admitted to all their rights.

Mr. Shellabarger of Ohio concurred in the necessity of taking precaution but he was not certain as to the best way of doing it. He offered a substitute for Mr. Farnsworth's resolution—appointing a committee of 9 (3 of the Senate and 6 of the House) to report on the subject at a future caucus.

Mr. Garfield of Ohio endorsed what had been said about the treachery of the President and the necessity of adopting some measures of precaution. He was happy to announce that Dennison had resigned and would have nothing to do with the Administration and hoped that other members of the cabinet would follow his example.

Mr. Boutwell of Mass. said he thought we should be obliged to do a good many other things to save the country from the danger that threatened it. A conspiracy was on foot to put the govt. into the hands of the rebels and the President was a party to it. He had no doubt they contemplated a resort to force, because it was in the logic of events that they should do so. He believed Andrew Johnson to be just as thoroughly a traitor as Jeff Davis and that nothing could save the country from destruction but the most prompt and effective preparation for every emergency. He believed an attempt would be made to force the rebels into Congress and the Phila Convention was part of the scheme. Any such attempt must and would be resisted by force. (Mr. Boutwell's remarks were loudly applauded.)

Mr. Kelley of Pa. said "amen" to Mr. Boutwell and said that many as were the letters he received from his constituents upon the tariff, they were few in number compared with those he received entreating him to stand by Congress in its measures for the salvation of the country. He denounced the Phila Convention as a conspiracy of traitors and said he believed the President had got it up for the purpose of destroying the Union Party. The rebel sympathizers North and South were in favor of it. The N.Y. News and World advocated it as a means of destroying the Union party and restoring the rebels to power. And the N.Y. Times, although it had not yet gone quite so far as this, also upheld and favored the convention.

Mr. Raymond of N.Y. said Mr. K. had not the shadow of right to attribute to the Times any such purpose as breaking up the Union party. He had his own views of the objects to be accomplished by the convention and he had not thus far concurred in the views expressed by those around him. He believed that properly managed the Convention would strengthen the Union party instead of destroying it. So long as he saw reason to think so, he should advocate it. Whenever he saw reason to believe that it was to be used to destroy the Union party neither the Times nor its editor would support it.

The resolution of Mr. Shellabarger was then adopted. Mr.

Stevens of Pa. offered a resolution declaring it to be the duty of every Union man to denounce the Phila. Convention and render it odious to the people. He said he wanted the lines distinctly drawn between the friends and the enemies of the Union cause and wanted it distinctly understood that no one who favored the Phila. Convention could have any fellowship with Union men.

Mr. Bromwell of Ill. followed in favor of this—denouncing the President and saying we ought to revise all the laws under which offices were created which the President can fill—and that salaries should be abolished and other means taken to render the power of appointment useless in his hands. Congress could sit all summer—*we were paid by the year and it made no odds.*

Senator Lane of Ind. followed in a very excited speech, demanding the enactment of stringent laws to restrain and curtail the power of the President,—saying he was ready to sit all summer if necessary at the point of the bayonet—that if a victim was wanted he was ready—and declaring that a million soldiers would flash to the Capitol to sustain Congress against the tyranny of the President. His remarks were received with applause.

Mr. Raymond of N.Y. said he presumed he was not guilty of any undue assumption in supposing the resolution was aimed in part at least at him. He regarded it as a menace, and so far as it was a menace he regarded it with contempt. He was not responsible, financially, professionally or politically, to the gentlemen from Penn., nor to the delegation from Penn., nor to the Union members of Congress. He held position in the Union party by favor of his constituents and by appointment of the National Convention. When either of these authorities saw fit to expel him, he would give heed to it. But the action of that caucus was a matter of entire indifference. When the Phila. Convention was summoned he believed it would have a good effect in nationalizing the Union party. He could never conceal his conviction that unless the party was thus nationalized it would be short-lived, and he had therefore looked with favor on the call for the convention. Whenever he saw reason to change his opinion as to its effect and object he should act accordingly, for a newspaper was compelled to discuss all the phases of public affairs as they arise.

He branded as utterly false and ludicrous all intimation that his action was prompted by a desire for office—saying that he would accept no office at the hands of the administration and asserted his purpose to be governed by his own judgment of what was wise and just.

The resolution was then adopted, Mr. Hale of N.Y. alone voting No and Mr. Raymond declining to vote at all.

The Chairman appointed as the joint committee to consider the question of adjournment the following gentlemen: Senators Chandler of Michigan, Morrill of Me., and Nye of Nevada: Messrs. Hotchkiss of N.Y., Farnsworth of Ill., Boutwell of Mass., Colfax of Ind., Loan of Mo., and Kelley of Pa.

The caucus then adjourned.

A second caucus was held two days later which was attended by some of the more moderate Republicans in the Senate and by certain members of the House who were worried about their political future in their local communities. The desire to remain in Washington indefinitely to guard against the possible treason of Andrew Johnson was not so pronounced as in the first caucus. Under date of July 14, 1866, Mr. Raymond recorded his impressions of the meeting:

The caucus of the two houses reassembled at the call of the Committee.

Mr. Conkling of N.Y. called attention to the fact that in spite of the injunction of secrecy the proceedings of the last caucus had been published in the N.Y. newspapers—but in so inaccurate a shape as to do gross injustice to individual members. He suggested either that the caucus should be open or that steps be taken to make the injunction of secrecy effective.

Mr. Raymond suggested that the subject be postponed for the present and that the caucus proceed under the rules adopted at the former meeting.

Mr. Stevens and Mr. Garfield concurred in this.

The Chairman called on the committee appointed on Wednesday for its report. Mr. Farnsworth of Ill. said that he did not see Senator Chandler who was chairman of the committee present. The Senator was in possession of the report of the committee but in his absence he would state its substance. The majority of the committee was in favor of continuing the session of Congress—or if that could not be carried—of the Senate at least through the summer. They had decided, therefore, not to recommend any time for adjournment.

Mr. Boutwell of Mass. said that he thought it very desirable that Congress should continue in session for other reasons than those which had been suggested. He would mention one. A distinguished gentleman from the South was in town from whom he had learned that the Louisiana Convention would meet on the 30th for the revision of the State Constitution and that amendments would be adopted disfranchising the rebels and enfranchising the loyal inhabitants without distinction of color. If Congress could be in session when this constitution should be adopted it could, in accordance with the precedent established in the R.I. case, accept it and thus give it validity as the Const. of the state. In the Rhode Island case the Supreme Court decided that it was for Congress to decide which was the constitutional govt. in any state in which doubt existed. If Congress should not be in session a long time must elapse before action could be taken, the new govt. of the state might fail to get a foot-hold and the country would experience a very serious calamity.

Mr. Ashley of Ohio said that to wait for the Convention to act would take us over to October at least.

Speaker Colfax said he would state the condition of the public business. We had still one of the appropriation bills to act upon. The Rousseau-Grinnell case of privilege was still undecided. The Soldier's Bounty Bill would come back to us from the Senate. A bill concerning the Judges of the Supreme Court was pending and there were several other bills of a good deal of importance still pending.

Mr. Washburne of Ill. said he was perfectly willing to stay if there was any necessity for it. But it was clear that it was not required by the condition of the public business as stated by the Speaker. He had known more bills of importance than the Speaker had enumerated to go through in a single night. As to the rather wild idea of sitting all summer to prevent the President from running the country, he hoped the caucus would not act upon any such motive. He moved that the caucus was in favor of adjourning on the 23rd.

Mr. Wilson of Iowa offered a resolution that Congress meet hereafter at 11 o'clock and that it is in favor of adjourning on the 23rd.

Mr. Morrill of Vt. said he was willing to remain in session if it would do any good. But he thought we could very easily finish our business and he was satisfied there was no necessity of sitting till December. It was clear that no rebel Congress could be brought into power before next March when this

Congress would expire. But after that he was satisfied that the rebels would be brought in by fair means or foul. But we can do nothing about this until the time comes. It was easy to see, moreover, that the Senate had no intention of prolonging their session—they are daily putting over business of importance until December.

Mr. Bromwell of Illinois thought the question of admitting Tennessee should be disposed of in some way before we adjourn. He was as much opposed to a "rump" Congress as anybody, but we ought to dispose of important public business.

Senator Sherman of Ohio was satisfied that the Senate could finish its legitimate business in a week, and a majority of that body was clearly opposed to sitting through the summer for any political purpose. There were two bills of a political character pending:—one to prevent removals from office by the President and the other providing for the admission of Tennessee. For his own part he would vote to admit the Tennessee members at once, with or without the ratification of the constitutional amendments, but others do not concur in this. Some insist that the state shall ratify those amendments, some that they shall become part of the Constitution, before the state shall be admitted. One thing is certain:—the President is no longer with the Union party. We must look this fact full in the face. Whatever he can do to destroy it, he will do. But in spite of that the Union party stands firm. In his own state, Ohio, it was never more compact and united than it is today. He did not fear anything the President could do against it. With or without his aid or that of any who were associated with him, the Union party can maintain its ascendancy. He thought Union members were needed at home to attend to the coming election.

Mr. Stevens of Pa. said that he could not agree with the remarks made by many gentlemen, nor could he concur in their views. Whence comes, he asked, this extreme anxiety, this unseemly haste to desert our post and abandon our friends to the tender mercies of the enemy? He was grieved to hear that the Senate which ought to protect the people against the machinations of the White House, was ready to adjourn. He had hoped that the people would be justified in looking to us as their guardians against the executive. How far our desertion of our posts would go towards breaking down the Union party he did not know, but one thing he did know—it would go very far to destroy the confidence of the people in Congress. He thought that if we could not make up our minds to stand to our posts, we need not be in haste at any rate, to adopt a resolution to adjourn—that we should remain in session as long as there was anything to do, and the longer the better. He did not believe we could do the business before us properly and deliberately in three weeks. He thought we ought not to think of adjourning until we passed enabling acts to authorize the rebel states to form constitutions on the principles of universal suffrage and of protecting loyal men and to enable them to organize state governments under them. He deemed such a law of far greater importance than all the others that had been mentioned. He hoped gentlemen would not act hastily on the subject of adjournment.

Mr. Price of Iowa thought it important that members should be at home attending to matters there. Congress can do little and the President can do nothing to injure the country until this Congress expires. We have no power over the thousands of small office-holders who are really the working politicians. He believed the President to be the vilest man that ever sat in that place and he would stay here and die if necessary to thwart his traitorous schemes. But he did not believe any good could be accomplished by staying.

Mr. Conkling of N.Y. thought it very important that

whatever Congress does in legislation should be done deliberately and with care—not under whip and spur as had been suggested by the gentleman from Illinois, Mr. Washburne. That was the very worst manner of legislating. He concurred entirely with Mr. Stevens in his view of the case. He hoped we would not meet at any other time than the usual hour, that we stay long enough to do all our business properly and then adjourn.

Mr. Farnsworth of Ill. offered a resolution that Congress would not adjourn until a law had been passed restraining the President's power of removal. But the previous question had been demanded by several members and it was not received.

The demand for the previous question was sustained and the provision to meet at 11 o'clock was stricken out. The resolution to adjourn on the 23rd then coming up,

Mr. Stevens of Pa. moved to lay it on the table. This was lost: and the resolution was adopted ayes 64, noes 40.

Mr. Raymond moved that the injunction of secrecy be removed from the proceedings of both caucuses.

Mr. Stevens of Pa. said he hoped it would be, that the people might see how indifferent Congress was to the public good. The resolution was then unanimously adopted and the meeting adjourned.

Reprinted with permission from the AMERICAN HISTORICAL REVIEW, *33:835–42, July, 1928.*

$\prec$ V $\succ$

UNIVERSITY
ADMINISTRATION

THE *years as administrator brought John Krout new recognition from his immediate associates and an ever-widening circle of admirers. As chairman of the department of history of the host institution, he introduced the president of the American Historical Association at the war-curtailed version of the annual dinner, held in December, 1943, at the Faculty House, Columbia University, with words so gracious and inspiriting that the Association paid him the unusual tribute of printing them.*

As dean of the graduate faculties, and later provost and vice president, he addressed himself to numerous problems of higher education. Here are his comments on four perennial topics: graduate training (in history), the role of research, the responsibilities of the alumnus, and the place of organized sports.

Introduction
of Nellie Nielson

A T the beginning of its sixtieth year the American Historical Association holds its fifth consecutive annual meeting in the lengthening shadows of a world at war. Here on Morningside Heights the naval training programs and other phases of the war effort go forward with no interruption. Some of you in coming across 116th Street may have found yourselves involuntarily falling into step with a platoon of marching midshipmen. Our classrooms and laboratories, as at other colleges and universities, are filled with men and women in the various military services. But if the university seems to be very busy at the moment with concerns which are not precisely those of the historian, it hopes that you will realize that its welcome is nonetheless cordial and sincere and that it looks forward with confidence to the day (not too far distant) when it may act as host to the entire membership of the Association.

Even with a drastically abbreviated program and the omission of many traditional features of these annual meetings, the Executive Committee believed that our purposes could be forwarded this year. It was probably mindful of Herbert Baxter Adams' wise comment: "The best results of a scientific convention are sometimes reached in conversational ways." There is, to be sure, no rationing which impedes the free exchange of ideas among us.

In this year 1943 the Association both celebrates an important anniversary and shatters a long-standing precedent. Fifty years ago the annual meeting was not held in December, but in July, in order that the two-day sessions might coincide with the World Historical Congress, sponsored by the Columbian Exposition in Chicago. On July 12 a professor of American history from the University of Wisconsin, who looked even younger than his thirty-two years, read a paper entitled "The Significance of the Frontier in American History." It would be interesting to know how many of the forty-nine members who signed the registration book at the time appreciated how far-reaching would be the influence of Professor Turner's words on the writers of American history. Certainly few of them thought that a half century later his thesis would still command the respectful attention, as Professor Pierson has so cogently demonstrated, of most of the historians interested in the development of the American nation. The report of the proceedings at Chicago seemed to place chief emphasis on a paper which discussed the origin of Virginia's House of Burgesses; while the correspondent for the *Dial* dismissed the meeting with the remark that "sensational theorists" had no place on the program. Even after the "Frontier" essay had been twice published, its Eastern readers could still describe it as an interesting but curious and very provincial point of view. There were letters of praise, however, from John Fiske and Justin Winsor, which inspired Turner's later quip that at long last he could "have faith in Massachusetts."

And that faith was not only in the Massachusetts of Harvard and Amherst and Williams but also in the Massachusetts of Mount Holyoke and Wellesley and Smith. My own most vivid recollection of Professor Turner calls up a conversation in which his eyes brightened with pleasure when he insisted that the founding fathers, needing a history of the Revolutionary struggle that would be at once realistic and powerful, turned to Mercy Otis Warren to supply what their own pens had failed to achieve. He would have applauded the decision of this Association in choosing, for its present leader, one who has nobly refuted the sharp dictum of testy John Adams that 'History is not the province of the Ladies.' At Bryn Mawr and at Mount Holyoke, in England and in America, her work is known for her rare gifts of combining the large view with the small one, of supporting the general concept with the minute examination of particulars, of illuminating great industry by knowing the goals toward which her task is leading.

It would be presumptuous for me to introduce Miss Neilson to this company. Rather may I present to her this representative group from the membership of the Association. We who have followed her along interesting paths which run through England's medieval economy will find it no less intriguing to accompany her on her intellectual adventures with the early pattern of the common law.

Ladies and gentlemen: The President of the American Historical Association.

Reprinted with permission from THE AMERICAN HISTORICAL REVIEW, *49:573–76, April, 1944.*

Administrative Problems
and the Need
for Exploring New Procedures

This was a contribution to a panel discussion with Dean Theodore C. Blegen of the University of Minnesota and Dean (later President) Elmer Ellis of the University of Missouri before the Third Conference on American History held by the Historical Society of Pennsylvania.

W E had rather agreed that we would try this afternoon to get you people to aim questions at us that would enable us to defend whatever positions we might want to take, or would clarify for us some of the things that are in your minds. I know that is always a difficult thing to do. May I try, therefore, to state some of the questions that are in my own mind and see whether you think they are important; if you don't, tell me about them in just a few minutes.

The first problem that bothers me a great deal is this whole matter of what we are working with in our programs of graduate training. I think it is really the alpha of our discussion. I am not talking now about whether or not we are getting students superior to those who go into law or medicine or the physical sciences. I am talking about whether the people who come to us saying that they have finally made up their minds to work in the field of history know why they want to work in that field and what they want to do after they have worked in it at the graduate level.

So many of them—and this experience I am sure is not peculiar to the institution which I happen to represent at the moment—don't seem to know what they are preparing themselves for, except in a very vague fashion. They talk to us often at the beginning of their graduate work still wondering whether there is anything else that can be done with history except to teach it. They raise that question, and I know they raise it elsewhere than at Columbia University, because I have had experience that proves to me that they do. It goes back to this whole matter, it seems to me, of what Dean Blegen called timing. They don't make up their minds often until pretty late in the educational process that they are going to try to do graduate work in history. Having made up their minds, they are a little bit uncertain as to what the future holds in store. They have a feeling that it would be nice if they could train themselves to be college teachers, or teachers in the graduate schools. But most of them also have a suspicion that they may end up their graduate work as teachers in high schools and other secondary schools, as they are called in this country— though why they should be called secondary, I have never been able to understand.

A good many of them have the feeling, when they come into graduate school and are told about research work and research training, that they are expected to go forward in research opportunities. They discover after a few conferences with their instructors that the research opportunities are decidedly limited. They discover that even those additional opportunities, which I think Mr. Powell was talking about, are more numerous than they used to be, but are still not numerous enough to take up more than a very small percentage of the men and women who are trained in our graduate schools. Consequently, they are thinking almost entirely, after a period of a few months at any rate, of graduate work in history in terms of teaching history, they hope in a liberal arts college or someday, perhaps, in a graduate faculty. Right there is the point where we fail them badly. We don't face that fact frankly, as Mr. Perkins told us this morning, and proceed to prepare them for the kind of responsibility they are going to have to assume when they complete what we call their formal graduate work.

I say that with all knowledge of the experimentation that is going forward, of the increasing emphasis that we are placing upon the training of college teachers, but I think we seldom talk to them about what college teaching can mean, what secondary school teaching can mean; and though occasionally we may discuss with them this whole matter of communication in a general way, I doubt that we very often spend much time with them pointing out that there are a variety of ways in which you communicate what you think you know to those whom you would like to instruct.

I would like to spend just a minute on that. I have personally been very much pleased that so many kind words have been said in this conference about the lecture method. I still think it has a place in teaching at the college level, as well as at the graduate school level. But you and I know full well that a great deal of teaching doesn't go forward on the basis of formal lectures delivered to classes, whether those classes are small or whether they are large. And if you ask yourselves about your own experience, it seems to me you will probably have a good deal the sort of experience that is my own. As I look back over my own training, it seems to me that I had three types of masterful teaching. One type was that which came from the inspiring lecture which showed me the way to get words across without mangling them. Whether I could follow it myself afterwards, I at least had an example of the way it was done.

Secondly, I learned a great deal in a small seminar group from instructors who never would have been— for I had a chance to see them in action in another way— effective classroom lecturers, but were magnificent men when it came to the matter of raising the vital questions that you wanted to discuss in a group of half a dozen or so.

Thirdly, and I hope you have all had the same experience, I have enjoyed some of the most effective teaching in my whole training experience from what I suppose would be regarded as a conference method or a tutorial method, in which you just talked to your instructor about things and discovered that the vistas that were opened up were almost greater than those which came from seminar work or from formal lectures.

Do we believe that those three methods of communication ought to be used in undergraduate instruction as well as in graduate instruction? There is a question I think that we need to ask ourselves about this whole educational process, for we have in many parts of it been compelled by force of circumstances to accept the doctrine that it is least costly to do it on the basis of the lecture method to large groups. We haven't felt we could, in terms of our social resources, do it so frequently in the other two ways. My plea would be that we see if we can't, in terms of our graduate training, persuade our students that they ought to become—I was going to use the word missionary, and I am not afraid of it—missionaries in the cause of helping our educational system to recognize and understand those three forms of instruction communication.

The second point is the matter not of whom we are working with, but of what we are trying to do with them. Sometimes they know, or feel they know, what we ought to be doing for them, and I think that we need in our graduate training to pay a little more attention to what they think they need. Why do you have to say to each man or woman who comes into graduate training, "You must take precisely this kind of program, because it is going to prepare you ultimately for the doctor of philosophy degree"? I am not talking now about those who after a few weeks in seminar make it plain that it is hopeless, that they will never reach that degree. I am talking about a great many of these people who have superior ability, but abilities that are not all alike. Some of them ought to be trained in one fashion and some in another, and I think it ought to be increasingly possible for us to do it in our graduate school programs, if not by the device of laying down alternative methods, then through the device of the kind of interpretation which intelligent faculty members and administrators ought to give to the rules.

One of my colleagues said to me only a short time after they asked me to accept the post of dean of the graduate faculties, "I hope you understand that your chief responsibility is to tell your colleagues when you are willing to break the rules." I suppose this is rank heresy. Probably Dean Blegen will throw me out of the fraternity for saying it, but I suspect that one of the things we need to do is not only to waive or suspend the rules, but occasionally to smash them into bits so they can't be put together again. This is particularly necessary for that particular man or woman who represents an ability that doesn't quite fit into the system, and who ought to be given a chance. This is a place where I like to think of freedom, and that is why I am not quite sure that our chairman of yesterday afternoon is entirely right when he says it is a "lockstep." It is in many cases, but it doesn't have to be that way.

One of the reasons why it has gotten to be a "lockstep," and I don't have to remind you of this, is the fact that we are trying to take care of an ever larger number of persons who come to us saying that they want to go on in graduate work specifically in the field of history. How many ought to be discouraged? I know a few of you are looking at me and saying, "Well, you ought to know; Columbia has gotten plenty of them." I don't know how many ought to be discouraged, because how can you know that until you know something about what the social conditions are going to be five years, ten years from now—what the needs will be? And when you are talking about needs, can you talk of them only in terms of the positions to be filled? How do you know whether we need more persons trained as we are training them for the Ph.D. degree in history? It seems to me we haven't yet the evidence. We probably have too many as of this hour—let's be frank about that—in a good many of our graduate schools, because we are carrying a much heavier load than we should be carrying with the personnel and equipment available. We have all said that it was a temporary thing, but temporary things have a way of becoming permanent, and that is the danger that faces us now. We are less than realists unless we face up to that fact. But when you ask the graduate school administrator to cut down by 100, 200, 300 next year in all of your graduate work, and to take twenty-five or fifty or sixty of them out of your graduate work in history, then you ask him to make decisions without his having the evidence. He doesn't know whether it is socially desirable to do it that way or whether it isn't. You people teaching the graduate departments of history have got to help us in determining where we should draw the line.

One more point I would like to make. Dean Blegen has made it, and since the assent seemed to be strong here, perhaps I ought not to make it again, but I would like to go on record as being most vehemently opposed to the proposition that the way to solve this question of what we are going to do with our graduate students is to separate those who are going to be teachers from those who are going on into scholarly research work. I think it would be one of the most disastrous blows struck at higher education in the United States if we adopted that kind of program. I don't need to labor the point with you, but you know full well that a great many of those outside the historian's guild or the guild of any of our scholarly groups sometimes have the impression that one of the first qualities of a good teacher is a healthy aversion to research work. It isn't true, and never has been. You must keep that vital connection; you are not going to train good teachers by separating them.

A few years ago Fairchild wrote in *The American Scholar* what I have always thought was one of the soundest articles on this whole question. In it he pleaded eloquently, and I thought persuasively, for a continuation of the doctrine that, although it places on a great many of our undergraduate teachers a pretty heavy burden, we must continue to insist that there be a connection between the kind of thing that makes for life in the classroom, that stirs the interest of the student, and the intellectual curiosity of the man or woman supposed to be stirring it. If we abandon the idea by saying, "All right, we will separate. There is a fork in the road. At this point you make up your mind: are you going to be a teacher or are you going to be a research scholar?" the emphases will vary. Certainly they will. You might say, "I am only taking that middle path," which is always the path of timid compromise. I don't believe that. I think it is essential that we keep these two things together.

Let's be honest about it. Are we then going to say, when we come to the matter of appraising the work of an undergraduate teacher, anything about matters of salary increase, promotion, relief from certain of the routine burdens that fall to all of us in terms of committee work, and so forth? Are we simply going to say, "Well, he hasn't written much; he hasn't been producing much; he isn't a very great scholar. He may be a pretty good teacher, but we get that largely on hearsay"? This is a point on which I happen to be out of sympathy, I know, with a good many of my colleagues in graduate school work. I think at that point it is time for someone to arise whose life isn't solely dedicated to teaching undergraduates in a liberal arts college, and to insist that consideration must be given to the type of person who spends a very large portion of his time in the fine art of communication, as opposed to the person who spends a much larger proportion of his time in trying to push out the boundaries of human knowledge through his own original curiosity or through an attempt to synthesize what others have found out before him.

Just one thing more. What are we doing in this content that we talk about when we say we are teaching graduate work? I hope we are doing something that has a purpose in terms of our own day and our own age, and I don't mean for one moment that we have to be present-minded about it. I wish we could persuade more of those who seem so concerned with the things of this present year and the years that lie immediately ahead that there is a great deal to be discovered about our present era by studying other periods in human history. I dare say that we can learn an enormous amount about this whole matter of the development of power in political life from the days of the Tudors, more so than we can by just focusing our attention on what we think has happened in Washington since 1933. And while you and I may say to each other that since we accept that, why parade the obvious by talking to this group about it, I assure you that outside of groups similar to this there is a great deal of questioning on that very point. The present-mindedness of a great many of those who say they are interested in what we are doing is the very thing that may ultimately, it seems to me, undermine our own confidence in the thing that we ought to be concerned about—the students and teachers of history. I am even inclined to insist that one place where we are failing these people who come to us for instruction is at the point where we refuse to commit ourselves as individuals on important moral and ethical considerations. We carry the idea of having to be neutral and objective in our training so far that we very frequently deny them, when they ask, "What do you think about that?" We evade and avoid, and I hope you will not think that I am unobjective and noncritical if I insist that we aren't going to train the kind of people whom we ought to be training as citizens of a democracy if we evade and avoid the crucial questions that they ask us about matters that certainly touch ethical and social decisions that they have got to make.

I have a feeling that there ought to be a content here that is more than just a content of bringing separate disciplines outside of history to bear upon these problems. Maybe I am old-fashioned about it. Perhaps this is reactionary talk. It isn't so, as far as I am concerned. I am prepared to experiment. I think we are beginning to. In the institution which I know best, we are cutting across departmental lines and faculty barriers all the time, and we are going to do more of it in order to see whether or not we can break down some aspects of specialization that don't seem to be bringing us as rich rewards as they ought to. But I also feel that we are in grave danger at times of refusing to face the issues about which these young men and women have a right to say to us, "You are a professor; what do you profess?"

Reprinted with permission from the PENNSYLVANIA MAGAZINE OF HISTORY, *74, no. 2:265–96, April, 1950.*

Education and Research

A S a student of history turned university administrator, there is nothing I can add to the excellent presentations which you have heard on the import for business and public policy of this unique investigation into the nation's human resources.

But coming last on this unusual program does afford me an opportunity to go back to the beginning and place before you some of the important lessons that I have been able to extract about research in the social sciences based on my close relations with the Conservation of Human Resources Project. We must not lose sight of the fact that our discussions this morning are the end product of a long and complex research undertaking—an undertaking that had to be established, financed, staffed, and directed before there could be any significant results for us to review today.

During the past five years the Conservation Project has provided me with an excellent vantage point from which to consider the potentialities and the perils of large-scale social science research under university auspices. May I share with you very briefly some of the important lessons that I have learned. For if we are to benefit more in the future than in the past from the results of research, we must act to deepen our understanding of its nature and put into practice what we learn.

The question might be asked: why do we suddenly need large-scale research in the social sciences with all of the complex problems that size always brings in its wake? Why can we not continue to rely on the individual investigator? In point of fact there always will be a place for the individual investigator who needs only a pad, a blackboard, or books. But there is no escaping the fact that much important research can be carried on only by a team of investigators, since no one man, no matter how talented he may be, can adequately master the relevant materials.

The current study is an excellent case in point. When General Eisenhower suggested the possibility of extracting from the rich repository of personnel records of World War II important lessons for management and the nation, he was quick to recognize that the success of such an effort would depend in the first instance on the ability of the university to organize a balanced team of experts. This is exactly what we tried to do. As you probably know, the key members of the Conservation staff were drawn from many different disciplines—from economics, political science, history, psychiatry, psychology, statistics, and social work. And throughout, the staff fortunately had as its senior advisor, General Howard Snyder, a physician with forty years' experience in the military service.

But I want to be quick to add that many specialists working on the same problem do not make a team. If each goes his own way, relying on his own specialized theories and techniques, many different facets of the problem may be illuminated, but the relations of the parts to the whole—the key to a deeper level of understanding —will still be missing. An effective research team requires each collaborator to contribute out of his specialty to the development of a unified approach.

This brings us to another challenge that large-scale research faces. The director of the Conservation Project, Dr. Ginzberg, has told me not once but on several occasions that in his opinion no one person working on his own could possibly have mastered all of the materials contained in "The Ineffective Soldier." Yet, unless they were mastered, nothing could have been produced. The successful resolution of this paradox depends on developing a method of fusing the best ideas of each collaborator into a unified approach. But synthesis must always take place in a single human mind. In the present instance, the director of the Conservation Project actually wrote (and this commands my admiration), with the draft materials of his collaborators to guide him, the entire three volumes.

Though team research is essential for a successful attack on many key problems in the social sciences, there are severe limitations in the university tradition that impede its full development. To begin with, the university —every university—is more or less severely compartmentalized. Each department or school is a small enclave in which the members are inclined to band together against all outsiders, especially all interlopers. They are no more friendly to the occasional colleague who wanders among several disciplines than some in the Pentagon look with favor upon the advocate of a unified service. It would be foolish for me to hide the fact that there are additional difficulties that the university faces in adjusting itself to large-scale research in the social sciences. Academic institutions have a long history of getting on with very little money. As you well know, the last decade has intensified the financial problems that they face because of the general inflationary forces that have characterized our economy and which have had such an adverse effect on university endowments and salary schedules. Poverty is not ennobling—at least not for the average man, nor even the average professor. The command over large research funds by a few faculty members frequently leads to jealousies and bickerings among colleagues and administrators. The battle for the dollar is by no means restricted to the banks of the Potomac.

If the university faces these and other difficulties in sponsoring large-scale research in the social sciences, why does it make the effort? Presumably, there must be important gains inherent in the relationship, gains alike for research and for the university. Let me call your attention to some of the more important.

While university faculties, as we have already noted, are staffed with men of feelings, it is probably no exaggeration to say that these feelings are more under control when it comes to the analysis and evaluation of data than among any comparable group of specialists. The university atmosphere is conducive to the objective and the critical. The professor is under no pressure, direct or subtle, to have his work confirm the judgments of the management.

I know that in recent years both the Armed Services and business organizations have begun to develop sizable research staffs to work on problems in the social sciences. In some instances they have been fortunate enough to attract very good men. And on occasion they have also sought to create the counterpart of an academic atmosphere in the hope of encouraging their staffs to exercise the full measure of their imaginative and critical faculties. All this is commendable and I would like to pay tribute to these sincere and honest efforts and to express the hope that they will be increased and multiplied.

But we may ask whether there are not inherent limitations as to how far a research team in a governmental or business organization can go if its findings begin to cast serious doubts on the wisdom of the management. After all, they depend on management for their jobs and their future. If the world were composed of managers as wise as Solomon and scholars as intrepid as Spinoza, there would be no serious problem in intramural research. But since the Solomons and the Spinozas are few, the advantage of university-based research over intramural research is real and it is likely to remain real for a long time to come.

There are additional advantages to locating important social science research at universities, or at least insuring that some of the key members of the group also hold staff appointments. I do not think it is accidental that men in both the physical and social sciences will frequently leave lucrative positions for a university post. This is particularly true for the man who is deeply committed to scholarly investigation. Why? The answer, I think, lies primarily in the unique opportunity that the university offers to combine research and teaching. No man, no matter how effervescent with ideas, can be continually productive. It is simply not possible for a person to explore continually on the frontiers of knowledge. It is exhausting work, and even the strongest man needs a respite now and again during which he restudies his strategy and regroups his forces.

There are several major advantages to the classroom. Perhaps the most important is that it provides the researcher with a respectable rationale during the period when he is lying fallow. It is very discouraging for the man who is exclusively involved in research to withstand periods of stagnation. He puts in time and has nothing to show for it. The university professor is automatically protected against such feelings of inadequacy. He can always gain some sense of accomplishment from his teaching.

The classroom has many other advantages. It provides, especially at the graduate level, an informed audience to whom the researcher can safely venture a preliminary presentation of his ideas. It is a basic fact of intellectual life that formulation and reformulation are essential if the tentative and imperfect are to be clarified and improved. I need hardly emphasize that students who are privileged to be members of a class where the professor is in the midst of an important undertaking will have placed before them new and often exciting materials and findings rather than the regurgitation of the old.

Here is one example. In the late 1930's the director of the Conservation Project had an opportunity to offer for the first time at Columbia an advanced course in "Economics and Group Behavior," in which he began very tentatively to explore new approaches to the study of human resources. The title of this course has changed over the years, but the important point to note is that there has been a reciprocal and constructive relationship between the director's teaching and his research.

There is yet another way in which research and teaching reinforce each other. Research is an ongoing process. It can be strengthened and expanded only as young men and women are trained. Some of the training goes on in the professor's own classroom, some goes on in other classrooms. During the past several years the emerging findings of *The Ineffective Soldier* were presented to students at the Industrial College of the Armed Forces, West Point, the Air Force Personnel Management Course, and to other military groups. They have also been presented before key management groups including the executives of some of America's most important corporations, such as Standard Oil of New Jersey, General Electric, du Pont, A.T.&T., Western Electric, and many others. The challenge to formulate the ideas that the Conservation staff were developing and the critical comments and suggestions which were received from these groups contributed significantly to the success of this project.

Then, too, there were presentations to academic and professional groups which served much the same purpose. I will refer only to the lectures which were given two years ago on the work of the Conservation Project at the University of California which were later published under the title *Human Resources: The Wealth of a Nation.*

Before leaving the subject of the university and social science research, I would like to stress one additional lesson that is clearly exemplified by the Conservation Project. No one group working by itself in isolation, be they professors, government officials, or businessmen, are likely to have the breadth and depth required to carry through a large-scale social science investigation all on their own. The specialized experience and skills of many different groups must be tapped. There is no easy formula for knowing how to do this tapping. But I am convinced that the success of social science research in the future will depend very greatly on the skill that we develop in bringing together the wide range of diversified interests that are required to advance the frontiers of knowledge.

Now in the few minutes that remain, I would like to place before you three considerations on which the future success of research in the social sciences largely depends. In each instance I will take my text from the Conservation Project.

The first relates to access to data. *The Ineffective Soldier* would never have gotten off the ground unless the Army's Chief of Staff had been willing to issue the following directive:

As a specific exception to the memorandum of the Joint Statement of Policy on the Release of Information from Medical Records of members and former members of the Armed Forces, dated 18 October 1949, and to current Department of Army policies relative to the use of military personnel records and other records in the files of the Department, access to such records will be authorized to designated representatives of Columbia University engaged in the project "The Conservation of Human Resources." . . . It is directed that individuals designated by Columbia University be given every assistance practical by all concerned.

And *The Ineffective Soldier* could never have been successfully completed had not the Director of Selective Service and the Administrator of Veterans Affairs likewise granted the Conservation staff access to confidential records.

There is no question in my mind that significant problems of major concern related to the welfare of the economy and the security of the nation can be successfully attacked only if we develop new and effective ways of releasing confidential materials to responsible research workers. Admittedly there are risks in such departures, but I submit that the risks are much less, on balance, than a continuation of the *status quo* in which materials which hold the answers to crucial questions remain under lock and key until they no longer have any value except for the antiquarian.

The second consideration deals with the mundane but ever important subject of money. I will remind you of what I emphasized earlier: universities are poor. Now I will add that large-scale research is expensive. It matters not whether the return on a research investment will be small or great; the simple fact is that no university has adequate funds to invest in research.

This brings us to an important point. Having postulated that large-scale research is essential and having just recognized that it is also expensive, and having further noted that no university is in a position to undertake the financing, we are left with only a few alternatives: foundations, business, government.

Not the least remarkable aspect of the Conservation Project was the fact that General Eisenhower succeeded in convincing business that it should provide the required financing, even though most corporations had up to that point shied away from supporting social science research, especially basic research. I do not want to draw too optimistic a conclusion from this single case, but I am encouraged that in the nine years since the Conservation Project was launched, a small but steadily increasing number of business corporations have been willing to make contributions to social science research, even where it is only indirectly related to their own immediate problems.

But the timidity with which business continues to approach the support of basic social science research brings me to my last observation about financing. Ever since the beginning of World War II, the Federal Government has been the major source of funds for research in the natural sciences, and it has recently become the dominant factor in the support of medical research. But to date, its contributions to the support of the social sciences have been extremely modest. Parenthetically, I want to emphasize that it *did* make a substantial contribution to the support of the Conservation Project, not in money, but in kind, by assuming responsibility for the processing of large bodies of statistical records and clinical case materials. There may be danger in recourse to the Federal Government for widespread support of research in the social sciences, but in the absence of real alternatives, I fear even more the dangers inherent in poverty and inaction.

This brings me to my third and final consideration. Research is a creative process. It depends for its success on the working together of a group of individualists. Unless each man is of strong and independent bent, he will be of little worth. Yet unless he can learn to work with others, the team effort cannot succeed. The creation of the proper atmosphere for such cooperative effort is exceedingly difficult; effective leadership is basic. But the team cannot pull itself up by its own bootstraps. It needs support and understanding from others.

Among the most important contributions of General Eisenhower to the Conservation Project was his providing at the outset that the team would have five years in which to test its approaches and show what basic research in human resources might accomplish. In point of fact it has taken the staff eight years to complete *The Ineffective Soldier* but during that time it has been able to complete and publish ten other books and monographs.

We are a pragmatic people, more interested in action than in thought, more concerned with today's accomplishments than with tomorrow's potentialities. But research is by its very nature geared to tomorrow. Time is an essential requirement. Unless people have time to think, they cannot produce. It requires not months but years to mold a team into an effective instrument for the discovery of knowledge.

The Conservation Project has underscored for me and I hope for everybody else that basic research in the social sciences is a long-term investment in which the only security for the capital is the integrity and intelligence of the staff. This is the lesson, above all others, that I hope management and the nation learns from Conservation of Human Resources Project that produced *The Ineffective Soldier*.

Reprinted with permission from the report of the Conference on the Ineffective Soldier: Lessons for Management and the Nation, 1959.

Noblesse Oblige: Alumnus
and University

*This was a talk delivered at Arden House in February,
1961, to representatives from thirty-three American colleges and universities, met to explore ways of creating a
"public consciousness and conscience among the alumni
of America." The conference, co-sponsored by Columbia and Southwestern at Memphis, was opened by
Dr. Krout, whose observations are reprinted in part here.*

ABOVE the desk in my study hangs a reproduction of
"The Michigan Creed." Signed by Alexander G. Ruth-
ven, once president of the University of Michigan, it
proclaims, in part:

We believe that the student should be trained as an
Alumnus from matriculation; for he enrolls in the University for life and for better or worse he will always remain
an integral part of the institution.

We believe that the relations between the alumnus and
his university should be beneficial to both, and that the
mutual assistance provided by the graduates and the institution should be limited only by their powers for service.

This concept of the relation of the alumnus to his college or university is general throughout the United States,

but one looks in vain outside this country to find its counterpart. In Europe there are a few institutions, in France and elsewhere, that have a rather anemic "Société des Anciens Elèves de l'Université," but these societies have little influence in academic affairs and, so far as is known, make no effort to raise funds for the universities with which they are associated. In South America it is common for the small groups of organized alumni to hold seats on the university governing councils and to participate—along with the students—in the election of the rector; but there is no tradition of continuing mutual service, and alumni feel no obligation to contribute to the support of the faculties in which they have studied. Nor can the close relation between the graduate and his college which has developed in this country be properly described in terms of the British "old school tie."

Why and how have our close relations come into being? The reasons are various. Perhaps one of them is the fact that for many generations our colleges and universities have thought of their students as unsophisticated pupils rather than as potential scholars. This may have been in George Ticknor's mind when, in 1816, he wrote to one of his Harvard friends from the University of Göttingen where he was preparing himself in German language and literature. "I cannot better explain to you," he remarked, "the difference between our University in Cambridge and the one here than by telling you that here I hardly say too much when I say that it consists in the Library, and that in Cambridge the Library is one of the last things thought and talked about." However well this intellectual gulf may have been bridged since Ticknor's day, it still remains generally true that American colleges and universities are interested in their former students as institutional representatives in various fields of endeavor rather than as members of the commonwealth of scholarship. The ties to Alma Mater have been and still are personal rather than academic.

On both sides this attachment has grown noticeably stronger as it became obvious that colleges, whether independent or tax-supported, needed alumni support. There is, it must be admitted, considerable justification for the oft-repeated alumni plaint that little attention is paid to them except when financial pressures rouse Alma Mater to action. Alumni activity, of course, did not begin in the last three decades; but the close cooperation of the colleges and their graduates has risen sharply since the days of the great depression. One need not labor the reasons for this development.

During the same period a change has been taking place in alumni attitudes. Over the country the conventional class reunions are less filled with adolescent emotionalism than was the case a generation ago. Graduates are manifesting, however self-consciously, more interest in the intellectual life of the institutions where they once studied. There is a decline, slight but noticeable, in the emphasis on athletics as the chief alumni interest. At this point, however, many college and university officials have frequently failed their alumni. Invited to meet with groups of former students, they seem to be afraid to talk about the main concern of the institutions they represent. Discussions of building programs, development plans, athletic achievements bulk large in their speeches. The educational process and its relation to the intellectual life of the nation receives attention, hesitantly, as a sort of last resort.

None will deny that the continuing education of the student, after the commencement curtain has fallen, is difficult. As Henry Wriston so persuasively argues, it requires remarkable skill and persistence; but in time it will bring worthwhile results, and there is a growing demand for it. If I may draw on our experience at Columbia, nothing in a long generation has encouraged us more than the response to the *Columbia University Forum*. It is widely read; it is read by alumni with critical insight; it has stirred discussion of important questions by persons with a high level of competence in their subjects. From alumni associations in other colleges and universities, it has won a recognition seldom accorded to similar publications.

Perhaps even more important is the increasing use of the panel discussion to present new and often divergent views. President Kirk and President McIntosh and some of their associates have moved out from Morningside Heights to Cambridge and Chicago, to Detroit and Denver, to San Francisco and Los Angeles, where they have talked about education, its content and its methods, in college years and beyond. While it is impossible to translate the lively spirit of such discussions into the printed word, the editor of the Graduate Faculties *Newsletter* deserves our commendation for presenting some of these conversations in these pages, so that thousands rather than hundreds may profit from them.

You may well argue that the examples which I have cited are, after all, mere episodes and fall far short of a thoughtful program of continuing education after graduation. Almost fifty years have passed since Hopkins at Dartmouth, Meiklejohn at Amherst, Embree at Yale and others emphasized the need for a new consideration of the mutual responsibility of the college and its graduates. Scores of institutions since that time have struck out along unbroken paths in search for a more satisfactory intellectual relationship with their former students. Last year Ernest McMahon reported on these experiments, comprehensivley and perceptively, in his *New Directions for Alumni.* The cumulative record which he presents is unquestionably impressive; yet unfortunately some programs have achieved less than the noise seemed to indicate.

Have we put our objectives, so far as education after college is concerned, into proper focus? What should we try to accomplish? Are we interested only in "refresher courses" to help alumni replenish their intellectual reserves? Do we wish to retain the former student indefinitely as an active member of the University community? Or are we really convinced that in this "age of the professional" the civic responsibility of the citizen is so great that he must continue his education after his college years—and that our institutions of higher learning must find ways to help him meet this heavy responsibility?

Surely any college or university that is true to its own ideals of teaching and research will not fail to give its students an attitude of civic awareness, even if it is merely —more often than not, one suspects—by a sort of intellectual osmosis. Implicit in the so-called liberal arts program is emphasis on the fact that no society, based upon the consent of the governed, can long endure unless the governed take an active part in public affairs. The perceptive student is well aware of the implication. For him or her it becomes a continuing influence. But not all are perceptive, and the awareness of the citizen's duty gained in college years quickly wears thin against the perennial abrasive of personal concerns.

Within the acquaintance of any one of us there are college men and women, not on any public payroll, who are unselfishly committed to the service of their fellows. Yet the list of such public servants fails to provide the civic leadership that this nation requires. It even falls short of what we have a right to expect, for from those who have received much our society should demand much. It is not enough for a college or university to boast —as so many do—about the number of successful doctors and lawyers, engineers and teachers that it has trained. One still may ask what contribution these highly favored alumni are making to the community in which they live and work. How much interest do they manifest in questions of public importance on which, as voters, they should have opinions—and on which their opinions frequently could be decisive?

This does not mean that the alumnus should be regarded as a member of an elite corps. Rather he should take his place as a responsible citizen who endeavors to do what he can for worthwhile public causes. Though this is not the specific end-product of a university education, surely it is a by-product so significant that it deserves more attention than most university teachers give it at the present time. The measure of our failure at this point is provided by the way in which thousands of university graduates avoid their civic duties—consistently, and apparently with a clear conscience. If college and university years provide no time for explicit teaching of the responsibilities that a democratic society imposes on its citizens, then a continuing program of alumni education on the subject may be the logical answer.

Each year, as I listen to the dean of the faculty of medicine administering the ancient and honorable oath of Hippocrates, to which the graduating class in medicine traditionally subscribes, I wonder how much thought the students have given to its ethical implications and how well they understand its social significance for themselves and the people among whom they will practice their profession. At the very least the oath is a recognition of the fact that fitness for the profession of medicine requires more than knowledge and special skill. It includes also a sense of moral values. Yet in an age that pretends to understand the social need for higher education, we seem to be hesitant, even fearful, of commitment to ethical principles. There is something profoundly disturbing about a society which rejoices in the high proportion of college and university graduates in the total population and at the same time condones almost anything from petty theft or cheating during examinations to malfeasance in public office or corporate conspiracy to defraud.

One example, perhaps, will suffice. The honest man who found unmarked bills, accidentally dropped out of a car, was generously rewarded for promptly returning the money to its legal owner; but his fellow-citizens broke his spirit with phone calls, letters, and telegrams telling him what a fool he was to return what he could have kept without fear of detection. The incident, of course, is an exceptional one; the mood underlying it, however, is pervasive.

As scholars we tend to assume that the magnificent scope of mankind's knowledge of philosophy, literature, art, history, and science is shot through with moral values which every student easily recognizes. As teachers, however, we pay little attention explicitly to these values, passing them by quickly in the classrooms or deferring discussion to some later time which seldom comes. If we are missing the chance to strengthen the moral fibre of our people during college and university years—and there is distressing evidence that we are—this could be the precise point on which a sensible program of continuing education of our alumni should focus. It is worthy of careful consideration by those who are convinced that "the mutual assistance provided by the graduates and by the institution should be limited only by their powers of public service."

From the GRADUATE FACULTIES NEWSLETTER *of Columbia University, May, 1961.*

Amateur Athletics—
Spectators or Participants

Excerpts from an address given at the 1959 Gold Medal Award Dinner of the Metropolitan Association, Amateur Athletic Union, May 6, 1959. Here Dr. Krout echoes his misgivings of thirty years earlier (see pp. 124–25) about the role of athletics in contemporary society.

I WOULD count it an honor to join with the friends of the Metropolitan Association of the Amateur Athletic Union on any occasion, but I regard it as a special privilege to be present when the purpose is to acclaim the imaginative work of Colonel Henshel for our common objectives. If this were a meeting in the early years of the AAU, we should be arguing, not always amiably, about the precise definition of the word "amateur." But that was true sixty or seventy years ago, and the decades since then have been filled with high resolve and equally high achievement. The record has been good, yet a good past can be dangerous, if it makes one complacent about the future.

If anyone can be complacent, in this day of tensions and anxiety, surely it is not the friend of amateur athletics. All the old doubts plague us and some new ones demand resolution. To be sure, it was thirty years ago that intercollegiate football had to withstand the shock of a distressing disclosure of overemphasis and professionalism in the forthright report of the Carnegie Foundation, and it successfully resisted its critics. But it was only a few months ago that the distinguished president of Yale made a clinical analysis of the "athletic scholarships" which no college administrator can easily brush aside. (Incidentally, the Johns Hopkins University seemed to be a singularly inappropriate place for such a critique of overemphasis on athletics.) Within the week an academic audience at Wofford College listened to a devastating description of the campus confusion inspired by our present system of intercollegiate sports. One often suspects that these indictments are overstated because those who draw them realize the reluctance of sports enthusiasts to accept any modification of a system which produces the colorful spectacles now so greatly admired. But, however exaggerated, the criticisms leave a sense of uneasiness among all of us who cherish the best in amateur athletics.

Have we really become a nation of spectators, watching rather than playing? Has "the passion for looking at and reading about athletic sports," which Lord Bryce remarked many years ago, finally culminated in making us a people who shun physical exercise, preferring to view sports spectacles from the comfort of an easy chair before the television set? For decades critics of the American scene have been making the charge that a steadily decreasing proportion of our citizens are participants in outdoor sports.

All the phenomena of "spectatoritis" have been obvious and well publicized—the crowded ball park; the building of ever larger stadiums to satisfy the largest spectator crowds since the gladiatorial combats of imperial Rome; the galleries of onlookers at every tournament, whether it be held indoors or outdoors. While all this became the domain of the statisticians, who could thus prove American decadence in athletic skills, a less spectacular growth of active sports was bringing about wider popular participation than any nation had ever known. It has been easy for critical commentators to see the "commercialism" in organized sport, to challenge the worth of the profit motive transferred to ball park, gymnasium, and playing field—and such commentary has proved to be salutary. But it is not mere complacency to recognize that one of the most significant developments of the last half century has been the growth of recreational facilities in our cities—playgrounds, athletic fields, softball diamonds, public tennis courts, and golf links. Here the urban workers, as well as the middle class and the fashionable world, have regained those opportunities for play which had actually been lost in the industrial changes of the nineteenth century.

In this truly democratic approach to one phase of popular recreation the Amateur Athletic Union has played its part well. Its emphasis has always been on the participant rather than the spectator, the amateur rather than the professional, the right of the many to play the games once reserved for the few. It can take pride in the steady rise of the amateur spirit at a time when organized sport seemed to have become highly professional and as complicated as "big business" in its structure and its regulations.

No sources exist by which one may measure the number of active sports participants; nobody really knows the precise proportion of our people who play basketball or tennis or softball or water polo; there are no accurate statistics on swimming in the summer or skiing when the snow lies right. Yet all the evidence we have points to two facts to gladden the heart of any amateur: (1) by mid-century Americans were spending far more of their leisure time—and almost five times as much of their money—on amateur than on professional sports; (2) this choice, freely made, was not controlled, ordered or regimented by any governmental authority.

The amateur spirit, exemplified by the AAU, embraces far more than active participation in sports on a broadly democratic basis. Its essence is *attitude* quite as much as *action*. This Union has striven—and with marked success —to make the way of the amateur athlete easier; to give him the fullest opportunity with a minimum of regulation. It has never insisted that the game should be played only for its own sake. It has always honored the winner. But it has also been quick to point out that its goal is individual excellence.

No team—and no individual—can win every contest. But every contestant can strive for the only thing that really counts, excellence in performance. Into every athletic event—whether it be on basketball court or cinder track, in swimming pool or baseball diamond— goes some measure of the skill of the performing artist. For the game well played is a work of art, as truly as any satisfying performance in theatre or concert hall. Here is the athlete's sure reward. He may not always win but he is poor, indeed, if he cannot after many a contest say: "Today I played my best and that best was excellent." Whenever we make an athletic award, are we not honoring the quest and the achievement of excellence?

At this very point athletics on the college campus too often fail us. The goal is to win the important intercollegiate contests. While there is nothing necessarily evil about the "will to win," it often gets in the way of the pursuit of excellence. That pursuit in some institutions becomes merely a search for young athletes, well trained in preparatory schools, who can be enticed by scholarships or other attractive inducements. It has little to do with a program of intramural sports that will give many students a sense of having learned to play some game well.

American colleges can be proud of the advances made in the last quarter century through the intelligent support of departments of physical education. Emphasis on intramural rather than intercollegiate phases of athletics have brought us much nearer to our goal of sports for all. Can we hold what we have gained? The test will come in the next decade. If costs continue to rise, while student enrollments soar, the pressure to curtail physical education programs may be irresistible. Make no mistake about it, intramural sports, properly conducted, are expensive. If our college leaders propose to expand these programs, at the very heart of amateur athletics, they may be tempted to use the device of financing them in large part from the receipts of spectator sports. The packed bleachers and the crowded stadiums may seem indispensable. And we could come full circle with all the evils of commercialism in "bigtime" intercollegiate sports being justified in the name of the amateur athlete. Here lies the danger that we may not have the wisdom to give the individual amateur the opportunity he needs, without sacrificing him to the pressures of neo-professionalism. Our colleges need financial aid on this front, as on many others. To the extent that they fail to receive it, the contribution which the Amateur Athletic Union has made and hopes to make to the preservation of the amateur spirit will be impoverished.

≺ VI ≻

THE FUTURE

JOHN KROUT *faced the troubled second half of the twentieth century with characteristic realism, faith, and educated optimism. He eloquently expressed some of his convictions in two moving addresses before the Columbia College Forum on Democracy, the first, February 10, 1949, the second, February 24, 1951.*

Why Talk about
Freedom?

A FEW months ago one of my colleagues here at Columbia was telling me of an incident which has impressive timeliness for us this morning. A young man in a Midwestern town had been employed to take a census of the
children within the community, and he was hurrying
toward the end of the day to get finished with his job
when he came to a house where the mother of a family
had just begun preparations for the evening meal. Some
of the children had been fretful during the day, she was
tired, she had work ahead of her, the doorbell rang, and
she had to go to meet this stranger who said he was taking
a census. You can imagine something of her irritation.
The young man asked her how many children there
were in her family, and rather wearily she said: "Well,
let's see, there's John, and Mary, Sue . . ." The young
man interrupted sharply and said: "No, no, no, I don't
want names, I only want numbers." To which the mother,
rather puzzled, replied: "But they ain't got numbers,
they've all got names."

That very commonplace incident throws the doors
wide open, it seems to me, to the most crucial question
of our generation, how do we propose to preserve in a

world that places more and more emphasis constantly on the social mass, the unique qualities of the human spirit? How are we going to be sure that when we talk about improving the condition of the group, we are also going to be able to save the people who compose that group?

The most miserable people in the world today, though it looks as if they were a very, very long time realizing it, are those who have carelessly exchanged their individual liberties for the tawdry trappings of a life in which they do not even have to think or speak for themselves.

Freedom throughout the ages, and you'll certainly hear this this afternoon from Professor Brebner, has been an inspiring word, and freedom itself is a glorious thing. We all love our liberties and our privileges. Why then talk about them? Why discuss them? Why not just enjoy them?

You'll have many answers to that question before Saturday evening rolls around, but one of the answers I hope you won't push easily aside—it is worth your while and mine—is to talk about freedom because for everyone of the liberties and privileges which you and I enjoy, there is a corresponding responsibility and obligation. William A. Dunning, who long ago taught history and political science on the campus here at Columbia, used to say with a merry twinkle in his eyes: "It isn't hard to find the American Bill of Rights, but Americans often find it extremely difficult to locate their Bill of Responsibilities."

Yet there is such a Bill of Responsibilities, in reality, whether it happens to be precisely defined in law or not.

Don't you suppose that was what the framers of the
Connecticut Constitution had in mind more than 130
years ago when they wrote: "Every citizen may freely
speak and write and publish whatever sentiments he
feels about all subjects, being responsible for the abuse
of that liberty."

There was a wide definition of freedom of speech and
of the press but with it an equally wide statement of the
responsibility involved. Wasn't it the same sort of thing
that the French had in mind when the authors of the
Declaration of the Rights of Man and of the Citizen insisted that "Liberty consists in the power to do whatever does not injure others." But where do you draw the
lines between that liberty which you desire and which
you think is beneficial to yourself, and that kind of license
which, perhaps pleasant to yourself, infringes upon the
liberty of others?

Now, there have been a great many persons who from
the beginning of human experience have written about
the boundaries of freedom, the beginnings of responsibility. And I would not for one moment this morning
have you think that I deprecate what's been set down in
political treatises, in excellent discussions of political
theory, in stirring pamphlets that deal with human rights,
but I submit to you that probably we Americans throughout our existence have learned a great deal more from
our practical experience than we have from reading
the writings of the great minds of the past. We owe
a tremendous debt to a whole host, and in that company stand men like John Milton and John Locke, Montesquieu and Rousseau, Grotius and Puffendorf, and so

many others, but is it by reading their writings that we take the measure of what we mean by freedom and responsibility in this land of ours? I'm inclined to doubt it. I suspect that the thing we need above all others, and you'll forgive me if I seem to say this just because I happen to have practiced the historian's craft for some years, what we need above all others is an understanding of our own past, for we've had, in many ways, a past that had led us along a different tangent than most of the peoples of the western world.

Perhaps the greatest thing in that past that caused us to deviate somewhat and to strike out along new lines was the fact of our overwhelmingly great natural heritage. We've added in our independent existence thirty-five states to thirteen little provinces clinging to the Atlantic coastline that actually won their independence from Great Britain. And of those thirty-five new states, all but six went through the territorial stage, learned the processes of self-government, found out by practice where freedom ended and responsibility began. And they did it on a stage the like of which human beings had really never seen before. Was there ever a people since the beginning of recorded history that had the kind of a theater on which to play this drama of democracy like the theater that the Americans from the end of the revolutionary era to the close of the nineteenth century enjoyed? Most of it was played, you know very well, in that magnificent valley that stretches from the crest of the mountain ranges that we call the Appalachians, and that valley represented an area that was greater than all of the empire conquered by the Roman legions in the days of the Emperor Trajan. In its eastern half alone, it was greater than all of Britain and the Netherlands, the German provinces and the Italian peninsula. The tributaries of the Mississippi carried every year a volume of muddy water to the Gulf of Mexico that exceeded all the water poured into the sea by the rivers of Europe, with the exception of the great Volga. The forest of hardwoods and soft woods stood ready to the pioneer's axe. Beneath its soil were riches of iron and coal and copper and lead and silver and oil which the mind of man had never comprehended. Don't you see that one of the greatest factors in determining our concept of liberty was the tremendous generosity of nature which had given us this magnificent area in which to develop our ideas about democracy: And those ideas were put to the hard test of practical experimentation. There are so many of them that I'd worry you if I tried to enumerate them this morning, but a few of them, I think, we ought to call to mind.

In the first place, we learned during the expansion across the great face of the American continent, to value highly freedom of thought, or call it freedom of opinion, perhaps that's better, which would ensure to us the fact that we could ever search without hindrance for the truth. We valued highly freedom of occupation or of enterprise, as some men call it, which guaranteed to us the fact that every man and woman would have an opportunity to move into any career where talent seemed to indicate. We valued highly freedom from arbitrary and oppressive government which made it possible for all of us to insist that there should be no compulsion upon the individual except by what we defined as "due process of law."

Those are some of the things that we learned through our experimentation. We didn't, or at least I do not believe that we got them, merely out of the writings of the great preachers of freedom in the past. They came to us as growth of the American soil, nurtured as they grew, to be sure, by men and women who knew something of the European tradition and what it had meant, but the nature of the fruitage that came was quite as much the result of the character of the soil and the environment in which they grew as it was the skill of the handicraftsman who cultivated it.

You see why I insisted that there ought to be no doubt in your minds about the desirability of talking in these next three days about freedom. You may say, "Well, what can I do by talking about it, how can I increase my own freedoms or learn to respect the freedoms of others?" If you don't talk about it in your generation, you aren't going to have it to hand on to the generations who come after you. Now is the time to talk about what's going to happen in the days of your children and your children's children. You will have opportunities to discuss phases of freedom, to look at its multitudinous aspects in the next few days. We hope you'll explore them carefully and thoroughly with candor and as complete an objectivity as you can possibly achieve. And, if you do, even though you may leave this conference saying: "Oh, there are so many questions that still remain unresolved; I didn't get the answers to lots of things that I took there in the form of questions," that's to be expected. But if you get from this some sense that you're the responsible agent, that your contribution to your community is the thing that's going to count in the next quarter century or so, then you've got part of the spirit in which this Forum was conceived and organized.

I think we could wish nothing better for you than if, during these next few days, you reach the conclusion that in order to resolve the questions of freedom and responsibility, you must have some sense of duty, something of a faith, some reverence for the laws you yourselves have made, some patient force to change them when you will, some civic courage, firm against the crowd.

Reprinted with permission from the First Columbia College Forum on Democracy, February 10–12, 1949, PROCEEDINGS, *pp. 8–15.*

Democracy's Endless Goal

Y O U R chairman has graciously conferred upon me a number of titles, but the one which I cherish most is that of charter member of the Forum on Democracy. Two years ago I had the privilege to be a participant in the first session, when Colonel Blackwell, Mr. Ingalls, Dean Carman, Dean Chamberlain, and others initiated the Forum. It is pleasant to join with you for this concluding session of the third Forum.

For so many of us today the "promise of the future" is heavily clouded with doubt, suspicion, and fear. The old, familiar guideposts no longer seem adequate in time of change, and we are convinced that the tempo of the whole historical process has been enormously speeded up in the last decade. Perhaps no generation of human beings has ever been quite so sure that it was participating in the closing of one era and the beginning of another.

As a result some have decided frankly to face toward the past and back reluctantly into the future, while others are inclined to forget the past entirely and to assume that the future calls for experimentation along novel, even fantastic lines. For these latter, not only the old guideposts but the very roads and fences are obliterated. Their "brave new world" will not be marred by any sentimental traditions; it will be unfettered by the burdensome chains of history; it will be inhabited by emancipated citizens who realize that the past is not only forever behind their backs but, indeed, quite obsolete.

I hope that you will not put me down as a stubborn reactionary if I insist that I have little faith in such a repudiation of our heritage. We can build nothing worthy of endurance in the years that lie ahead, unless we are ready to use the great spiritual resources that have come to us out of the Hebraic-Christian ethic through the traditions of Graeco-Roman culture.

So much that is precious in what we call Western civilization is our direct inheritance from that ethic that all of it cannot be stated even sketchily in these brief remarks. But, perhaps, we can fix our attention on one of the qualities which over the last century and a half has caught and held the spirit of man. Even in these days of disillusionment and doubt it will not let him go.

By the closing decades of the eighteenth century, Americans were convinced that one of the things they wanted most was individual liberty. At first their idea of liberty had been merely the protest of malcontents who had left the Old World because of economic oppression, political tyranny, or religious attitudes that they didn't happen to like. It took them quite a while after they got over here before they began to grope toward an awareness of the fact that democracy wasn't a system, that it wasn't a dogma, that it wasn't a theoretical philosophy. It was a way of living your life. And it offered you ideal goals which would probably almost always be beyond your grasp, but would, thereby, lengthen the reach of everyone of you.

Some writers today talk about democracy as if there were a Golden Age when it existed in the Western world. Now it has declined, and we live in an age of brass and iron and that Golden Age of democratic thinking and democratic action is behind us. No fiction could be farther from the truth.

It is outrageous for any of us to talk or think that way about the fundamental principles of the democratic life. We have only tried them for a brief period. We have them today in mid-twentieth century in a vigorous form around us, more vigorous than they've ever been before. Are we going to allow a few clouds that hang over us, because certain challenges have arisen, to weaken our faith, to drive us away from the kind of testing that's been the glory of the American people from the days the first Europeans set foot on the North American continent? You know, as well as I do, that one of the things basic in this whole ideal of democracy toward which we move—however haltingly and fumblingly—is the ideal of the liberty of the individual. And we now stand with the countries of the Western world—unless we've grown weary in the kind of thing we've been working toward for more than 150 years now in this country—we stand on the verge of realizing a greater degree of liberty for the individual under law than we've ever known before. It isn't something that's written in the political treatises. It's the kind of thing that we experience every day of our lives; and we don't know it unless we experience it.

You can read so much about it, you can learn the clichés and the phrases that express it, but you'll never come near having it unless you're prepared to experience it in your daily living. I challenge you to think of it in terms of your own actions and your own beliefs.

You can say with Thomas Jefferson, as he wrote many years ago to his friend, DuPont de Nemours in France at the time of the French Revolution: "You and I both love the people, but you love them as children whom you fear to trust without their nurses. I love them as adults whom I freely lead to self-government." You can say that with Thomas Jefferson and believe it; but it is meaningless unless you are prepared to translate it into the action of your daily lives. And translating it into action means doing something more than most of us are doing at the present time. You have heard during this Forum, and rightly so, a great deal about public policy, about national affairs, about foreign policy and international affairs. All of that is vastly important, for you are the ones ultimately who have to help make the decisions in those fields. But we might just as well be honest with each other. It isn't given to many of us, even in this company, to participate on such a high level of determination of policy that we can feel we really influence much the course of events one way or another. But it is given to each one of us to live the life that the democratic ideal requires of us day in and day out, week after week; and that's the kind of thing I challenge you with today.

If you'll pardon a very personal comment, it was only

a few years ago that I had a chance to have a reunion with an admiral in the American navy who had been my schoolmate chum in the days when I was going through grammar school. I hadn't seen him for a great many years. In the intervening time he had gone through the First World War and the Second World War with great distinction. In the course of our talk that evening I said to him: "What do you think of the young men that you served with in this Second World War?" He thought a little while and then he said: "They're a grand lot. They've got a magnificent sense of their obligation in great affairs." He said they had the courage to face any crisis. They were willing to move right in even though many of them felt it meant death. They didn't fail anybody there. "But," he said, "I often thought they lacked just a little bit of what I like to call the courage of the commonplace. They flunked little things in life that seemed to them rather insignificant and unimportant. They were tough and disciplined aboard ship, when we moved into action or when any emergency was at hand. They died gloriously; but they didn't always live with the same courage that they showed when the crisis was at hand." Isn't that indicative of one of the things that faces us, the fact that it's rather easier for almost all of us to be courageous when the stress is great and the moment itself seems historic? It's awfully hard to show in our everyday relationships the kind of courageous defense of democratic principles, the tolerance of the other fellow who happens to disagree honestly and in good faith, the will to sacrifice our individual desire for what we know full well may be the social good. All of these require a courage that often transcends the courage of the crisis.

But I haven't much doubt about you and your generation. It's a younger generation than mine. I'm here to say I think it's a better generation in many respects than mine. It will achieve great things in this twentieth century. It will achieve great things in this "decade of decision," as General Eisenhower likes to call the times immediately ahead of us, when so many things seem at stake, if it insists upon maintaining those freedoms which have always undergirded our democratic idea: *freedom of conscience,* that we may test the moral foundations of our laws and institutions; *freedom of thought,* that we may be unhampered in our hopeful search for the truth; *freedom of enterprise,* that we may have the right to seek the calling which talent seems to indicate; *freedom from arbitrary government,* so that we be not oppressed except by laws which follow the procedures of due process of law.

I think I have a right to say to you members of this Forum that you really have no business in this company unless you're filled by the spirit that caused Stephen Vincent Benét to cry out during the last war: "There's a buried thing in all of us, deeper than all the noise of the parade, a thing the haters never understand and never will, the habit of the free." That habit of the free is a precious thing to those of us who have the happy opportunity to live in the twentieth century, in the light of the traditions of Western civilization. It's ours to carry forward, if we continue to strive toward the things that we know are democratic ideals. One era ends, another begins, and the years roll, but democracy is everything if it stands for an endless goal.

Reprinted with permission from the Third Columbia College Forum on Democracy, February 22–24, 1951, PROCEEDINGS, *p. 34–37.*

Bibliography

BOOKS

The Adventure of the American People; a History of the United States (with Henry F. Graff). New York, Rand McNally, 1959. Revised ed., 1963. 738p. (Rand McNally social studies).

American History for Colleges (with David Saville Muzzey). Boston, New York, etc., Ginn and Company, 1933. 872p. (Other editions: 1938, 890p., and 1943, 961p.).

Annals of American Sport. New Haven, Yale University Press, 1929. 360p. (The Pageant of America, v. 15).

The Completion of Independence, 1790–1830 (with Dixon Ryan Fox). New York, Macmillan, 1944. 487p. (A History of American Life, v. 5)

A Course for Home Students in Modern European History (with J. Lloyd Mecham). New York, Columbia University, 1923. 69p.

A Course for Home Students in Modern European History, 1500–1789: The Old Régime (with John H. Wuorinen). New York, Columbia University Press, 1927. 65p.

The Greater City: New York, 1898–1948, edited by Allan Nevins and John A. Krout. New York, Columbia University Press, 1948. 260p.

The Origins of Prohibition. New York, Alfred A. Knopf, 1925. 339p. (Published also as Columbia University Ph.D. thesis).

An Outline History of the United States since 1865. New York, Barnes and Noble, 1933. 197p. (College outline series). (Published under this title through the 6th ed., 1941, 230p.; beginning with the 1st (i.e., 7th) ed., 1946, 246p., through the 5th (i.e., 11th) ed., 1951, 264p., published under the title, *New Outline-History of the United States since 1865;* the 12th ed., 1953, 270p., through the 14th ed., 1960, 278p., appeared under the title, *United States since 1865.*)

An Outline History of the United States to 1865. New York, Barnes and Noble, 1933. 163p. (College outline series). (Published under this title in a revised edition, 1935, 165p., and 3d ed., 1940, 165p.; a newly revised edition, 1946, 210p., was published under the title, *New Outline-History of the United States to 1865;* the 4th ed., 1953, 210p., and 5th ed., 1955, 210p., were published under the title, *United States to 1865.*)

An Outline of the Middle Period of American History (with Roy Franklin Nichols) . . . prepared especially for home students. New York, Columbia University, 1926. 74p.

A Syllabus for the General Course in American History (with Roy Franklin Nichols) . . . with an introduction to historical method, by Dixon Ryan Fox. New York, Columbia University, 1923. 116p.

PARTS OF BOOKS

"The American Bill of Rights." In Institute for Religious and Social Studies, Jewish Theological Seminary of America. *Great Expressions of Human Rights* . . . edited by R. M. MacIver. New York, The Institute; distributed by Harper, 1950. p. 135–43.

"Democracy's Endless Goal." In Columbia College Forum on Democracy, 3d, 1951. *Proceedings,* February 22–24,

1951. New York, Columbia University, Columbia College, 1951? p. 34–37.

"Education and Research." In Conference on "The Ineffective Soldier," Washington, D.C., 1959. *Conference . . . "The Ineffective Soldier": Lessons for Management and the Nation.* Sponsored by the Department of the Army, 30 June 1959. Washington, D.C., 1959. p. 17–20.

"Finance and Army Supplies." In *History of the State of New York,* edited by Alexander C. Flick. v. 4, *The New State.* New York, Columbia University Press, 1933. p. 113–48.

"Framing the Charter." In *The Greater City: New York, 1898–1948,* edited by Allan Nevins and John A. Krout. New York, Columbia University Press, 1948. p. 41–60.

"Reflections of a Social Historian." In William Ezra Lingelbach, ed., *Approaches to American Social History.* New York, London, Appleton-Century, 1937. p. 57–79.

"Sports and Recreation" (with Clifford L. Lord). In *History of the State of New York,* edited by Alexander C. Flick. v. 10, *The Empire State.* New York, Columbia University Press, 1937. p. 215–54.

"Why Talk about Freedom?" In Columbia College Forum on Democracy, 1st, 1949. *Proceedings,* February 10–12, 1949. New York, Columbia University, Columbia College, 1949. p. 8–15.

CONTRIBUTIONS TO
ENCYCLOPEDIAS, ETC.

Dictionary of American Biography. New York, Scribner, 1928–37.

Livingston, Peter Van Brugh, 11:315–16; Livingston, Philip, 11:316–18; Livingston, Robert, 11:318–19; Livingston, William, 11:325–27; Morris, Lewis (1671–1746),

13:213–14; Morris, Lewis (1726–1798), 13:214–15; Morris, Richard, 13:218–19; Morris, Robert (1745–1815), 13:223–24; Morris, Robert Hunter, 13:225–26; Raines, John, 15:326–27; Schuyler, George Washington, 16:472–73; Schuyler, Margarita, 16:475; Schuyler, Philip John, 16:477–80; Van Cortlandt, Philip, 19:162–63; Van Cortlandt, Pierre, 19:163–64; Van Cortlandt, Stephanus, 19:164–65.
Encyclopedia of the Social Sciences. New York, Macmillan, 1930–35.
Dow, Neal, 5:229–30.

CONTRIBUTIONS TO PERIODICALS

"Administrative Problems and the Need for Exploring New Procedures" (with Theodore C. Blegen and Elmer Ellis). In Historical Society of Pennsylvania, Conference on American History, 3d. *Graduate Training Problems in History.* Philadelphia, 1950. *Pennsylvania Magazine of History,* 74, no. 2:265–96, April, 1950.
"Alexander Hamilton's Place in the Founding of the Nation." American Philosophical Society. *Proceedings,* 102:124–28, April, 1958.
"American Political History." *American Year Book.* 1925, p. 1–31; 1926, p. 17–27; 1927, p. 1–8, 97–99.
"Behind the Coat of Arms; a Phase of Prestige in Colonial New York." *New York History,* 16:45–52, January, 1935.
"Dixon Ryan Fox." *Westchester County Historical Bulletin,* 25:128–31, October, 1949.
"Franklin's Contribution to the Constitution." *Outlook,* 145:256 (cover), February 23, 1927.
"The Genesis and Development of the Early Temperance Movement in New York State." New York State Historical Association. *Quarterly Journal,* 4:78–98, April, 1923.

"Glimpses of a Golden Age." *American Mercury*, 5:208–14, June, 1925.

"Hamilton's Contribution to the Constitution." *Outlook*, 145:193, February 16, 1927.

"Henry J. Raymond on the Republican Caucuses of July 1866." *American Historical Review*, 33:835–42, July, 1928.

Introduction of Nellie Neilson, President of the American Historical Association, 58th Annual Meeting, New York, December 29–30, 1943. *American Historical Review*, 49:573–76, April, 1944.

"Jefferson's Contribution to the Constitution." *Outlook*, 145:288 (cover), March 2, 1927.

"Lincoln's Contribution to the Constitution." *Outlook*, 145:416 (cover), March 30, 1927.

"Madison's Contribution to the Constitution." *Outlook*, 145:320 (cover), March 9, 1927.

"The Maine Law in New York Politics." *New York History*, 17:260–72, July, 1936.

"The Making of the Pageant of America." *Historical Outlook*, 22:103–7, March, 1931.

"Marshall's Contribution to the Constitution." *Outlook*, 145:352 (cover), March 16, 1927.

"New York's Early Engineers." *New York History*, 26:269–77, July, 1945.

"The Next Half Century." Middle States Council for the Social Studies. *Proceedings*, 50:13–16, 1953.

"Noblesse Oblige: Alumnus and University." Columbia University *Graduate Faculties Newsletter*, May, 1961, p. 1–3. Excerpts from an address at a conference on "public consciousness among alumni" held at Arden House, February, 1961.

"Report of the Committee on History." National Advisory Council on Radio in Education. *Proceedings*, 1:216–18,

1931. (Proceedings of 1st assembly called *Radio and Education*).

"Some Reflections on the Rise of American Sport." Association of History Teachers of the Middle States and Maryland. *Proceedings of the Meeting* . . . *1928*, no. 26:84–93, 1929.

The Ticonderoga Meeting of the New York State Historical Association. *New York History*, 15:6–16, January, 1934.

"The Washington Legend." *New York Times Book Review*, July 1, 1945, p. 3, 17.

"Washington's Contribution to the Constitution." *Outlook*, 145:173–74, February 9, 1927.

"Webster's Contribution to the Constitution." *Outlook*, 145: 384 (cover), March 23, 1927.

SERIAL PUBLICATIONS EDITED

Academy of Political Science, New York. *Proceedings*. Editor, v. 17, no. 2–v. 25, no. 2 (January, 1937–January, 1953).

Political Science Quarterly, a Review Devoted to the Historical, Statistical and Comparative Study of Politics, Economics and Public Law. Managing Editor, v. 51, no. 4—v. 68, no. 1 (December, 1936—March, 1953).

BOOK REVIEWS

Adams, Henry. *The Formative Years: A History of the United States during the Administrations of Jefferson and Madison*. Condensed and edited by Herbert Agar. Boston, Houghton Mifflin, 1947. *American Historical Review*, 53: 555–56, April, 1948.

Adams, James Truslow, ed. *Album of American History*. v. II, *1783–1853*. New York, Scribner, 1945. *New York Herald Tribune Weekly Book Review*, September 16, 1945, p. 2.

Adams, John Quincy. *The Selected Writings of John Quincy Adams*. Edited and with an introduction by Adrienne Koch and William Peden. New York, Knopf, 1946. *New York Times Book Review*, October 20, 1946, p. 4.

Beard, Charles Austin. *The Republic*. New York, Viking, 1943. *New York Times Book Review*, October 3, 1943, p. 3.

Bishop, Morris. *Champlain, the Life of Fortitude*. New York, Alfred A. Knopf, 1948. *New York Times Book Review*, November 7, 1948, p. 4.

Bonsal, Stephen. *When the French Were Here; a Narrative of the Sojourn of the French Forces in America, and Their Contribution to the Yorktown Campaign. . . .* Garden City, N.Y., Doubleday, Doran, 1945. *New York Times Book Review*, July 15, 1945, p. 21.

Bowers, David Frederick, ed. *Foreign Influences in American Life; Essays and Critical Bibliographies*. Edited for the Princeton Program of Study in American Civilization. Princeton, Princeton University Press, 1944. *New York Times Book Review*, September 30, 1945, p. 16.

Brinton, Clarence Crane. *From Many, One; the Process of Political Integration, the Problem of World Government*. Cambridge, Harvard University Press, 1948. *Saturday Review of Literature*, 31:14, May 15, 1948.

Bryan, William Alfred. *George Washington in American Literature, 1775–1865*. New York, Columbia University Press, 1952. *American Historical Review*, 59:134–35, October, 1953.

Caldwell, Robert Granville. *A Short History of the American People, 1492–1860*. New York, Putnam, 1925. *Historical Outlook*, 17:135–36, March, 1926.

Christman, Henry. *Tin Horns and Calico; a Decisive Epi-*

sode in the Emergence of Democracy. New York, Henry
Holt, 1945. *New York Times Book Review,* March 18,
1945, p. 5.

Coulter, Ellis Merton. *The Civil War and Readjustment in
Kentucky.* Chapel Hill, University of North Carolina
Press, 1926. *Historical Outlook,* 18:392–93, December,
1927.

Crane, Verner Winslow. *Benjamin Franklin, Englishman and
American.* Baltimore, Williams and Wilkins, 1936. *American Historical Review,* 42:736–88, July, 1937.

Cunz, Dieter. *The Maryland Germans, a History.* Princeton,
Princeton University Press, 1948. *New York Times Book
Review,* October 30, 1949, p. 44.

Curti, Merle Eugene. *The American Peace Crusade, 1815–
1860.* Durham, Duke University Press, 1929. *Historical
Outlook,* 21:398, December, 1930.

Faÿ, Bernard. *The Two Franklins; Fathers of American
Democracy.* Boston, Little, Brown, 1933. *American Historical Review,* 39:741–42, July, 1934.

Fish, Stuyvesant. *1600–1914.* New York, privately printed,
J. J. Little and Ives Company, 1942. *New York History,*
24:283–84, April, 1943.

Franklin, Benjamin. *Benjamin Franklin's Own Story; His
Autobiography Continued from 1759 to His Death in
1790, with a Biographical Sketch Drawn from His
Writings,* by Nathan G. Goodman. Philadelphia, University of Pennsylvania Press, 1937. *American Historical
Review,* 44:209, October, 1938.

Friedman, Lee Max. *Jewish Pioneers and Patriots.* New York,
Macmillan, 1943. *American Historical Review,* 50:161,
October, 1944.

Goodman, Nathan Gerson. *Benjamin Rush, Physician and
Citizen, 1746–1813.* Philadelphia, University of Pennsyl-

vania Press, 1934. *American Historical Review*, 41:196–97, October, 1935.

Gordon, Manya. *How to Tell Progress from Reaction; Roads to Industrial Democracy*. New York, Dutton, 1944. *New York Times Book Review*, October 8, 1944, p. 5.

Hale, William Harlan. *The March of Freedom; a Layman's History of the American People*. New York and London, Harper, 1947, *New York Herald Tribune Weekly Book Review*, May 18, 1947, p. 14.

Hatcher, William B. *Edward Livingston: Jeffersonian Republican and Jeffersonian Democrat*. University, La., Louisiana State University Press, 1940. *New York History*, 22:221–23, April, 1941.

Hebert, Walter H. *Fighting Joe Hooker*. Indianapolis, Bobbs-Merrill, 1944. *New York Times Book Review*, December 24, 1944, p. 7.

Humphrey, Edward Frank. *An Economic History of the United States*. New York, Century, 1931. *American Historical Review*, 37:350–51, January, 1932.

Kieran, John. *The American Sporting Scene*. New York, Macmillan, 1941. *New York History*, 23:219–20, April, 1942.

Kirkland, Edward Chase. *The Peacemakers of 1864*. New York, Macmillan, 1927. *Historical Outlook*, 19:91, February, 1928.

Kraus, Michael. *The Atlantic Civilization; Eighteenth-century Origins*. Published for the American Historical Association. Ithaca, Cornell University Press, 1949. *New York Times Book Review*, February 5, 1950, p. 10.

Lafayette, Marie Joseph Paul. *The Letters of Lafayette to Washington. 1777–1799*, edited by Louis Gottschalk. New York, privately printed by Helen F. Hubbard, 1944. *New York Times Book Review*, June 10, 1945, p. 7.

Levin, Peter R. *Seven by Chance; the Accidental Presidents.* New York, Farrar, Straus, 1948. *New York Times Book Review,* June 20, 1948, p. 3.

McGuire, Paul. *Experiment in World Order.* New York, Morrow, 1948. *Saturday Review of Literature,* 31:14, May 15, 1948.

Martin, Asa Earl. *History of the United States,* v. 1, *1783–1865.* Boston, Ginn and Company, 1928. *American Historical Review,* 34:609–11, April, 1929.

———— v. 2, *1865–1931.* Boston, Ginn and Company, 1931. *American Historical Review,* 38:387, January, 1933.

Mearns, David Chambers. *The Lincoln Papers; the Story of the Collection.* Garden City, N.Y., Doubleday, 1948. *Yale Review,* n.s., 38:346–49, Winter, 1949.

Miller, John Chester. *Triumph of Freedom, 1775–1783.* Boston, Little, Brown, 1948. *New York Times Book Review,* May 16, 1948, p. 12, 14.

Morris, Richard Brandon. *Government and Labor in Early America.* New York, Columbia University Press, 1946. *New York Times Book Review,* June 2, 1946, p. 22.

Mowry, George Edwin. *Theodore Roosevelt and the Progressive Movement.* Madison, University of Wisconsin Press, 1946. *New York Times Book Review,* July 14, 1946, p. 7.

Nolan, James Bennett. *General Benjamin Franklin; the Military Career of a Philosopher.* Philadelphia, University of Pennsylvania Press, 1936. *American Historical Review,* 42:786–88, July, 1937.

Ryan, Lee Winfree. *French Travelers in the Southeastern United States, 1775–1800.* Bloomington, Ind., Principia Press, 1939. *American Historical Review,* 46:222, October, 1940.

Salmon, Lucy Maynard. *Why Is History Rewritten?* New

York, Oxford University Press, 1929. *Historical Outlook,* 21:336, November, 1930.

Schachner, Nathan. *Alexander Hamilton.* New York, London, Appleton-Century, 1946. *New York Times Book Review,* June 16, 1946, p. 6.

Schlesinger, Arthur Meier. *The American as Reformer.* Cambridge, Harvard University Press, 1950. *American Historical Review,* 57:686–87, April, 1952.

—— *Learning How to Behave; a Historical Study of American Etiquette Books.* New York, Macmillan, 1946. *New York History,* 29:82–84, January, 1948.

Schlesinger, Arthur Meier, Jr. *The Age of Jackson.* Boston, Little, Brown, 1945. *Yale Review,* n.s., 35:727–29, Summer, 1946.

Smith, Edward Conrad. *The Borderland in the Civil War.* New York, Macmillan, 1927. *Historical Outlook,* 19:40, January, 1928.

Still, Bayrd. *Mirror for Gotham; New York as Seen by Contemporaries from Dutch Days to the Present.* New York, University Press, 1956. *American Historical Review,* 62: 930–31, July, 1957.

Styron, Arthur. *The Last of the Cocked Hats; James Monroe and the Virginia Dynasty.* Norman, University of Oklahoma Press, 1945. *New York Times Book Review,* January 27, 1946, p. 6.

Wertenbaker, Thomas Jefferson. *The Golden Age of Colonial Culture.* New York, New York University Press, 1942. *New York History,* 24:438–40, July, 1943.

Wiltse, Charles Maurice. *John C. Calhoun.* v. 1, *Nationalist, 1782–1828.* Indianapolis, Bobbs-Merrill, 1944. *New York Times Book Review,* November 5, 1944, p. 5.